Institutional Equities and the Broker Dealer

An Introduction

Michael J. Green

Copyright © 2014 Mr. Michael J. Green
All rights reserved.

ISBN: 1500939137
ISBN 13: 9781500939137

One

Foreword

About 10 years ago, I started work in the securities industry and back then I really knew nothing about what I was getting myself into. Sure, I knew the basics such as what stocks and bonds were, but I had no idea what these products were really about. Over the years I acquired this knowledge and looking back on those early days I wish that I could have had a book that explained the basics to me. It was with this in mind that I wrote this book.

This book was written to help people new to the industry, or those interested in the industry, gain an understanding of what we actually do. However, since this book covers a lot of products, those working in the industry will also find it useful as a reference.

This book contains the following content:

1. It begins with a general high level explanation of what investment banks are and what they do.
2. Then we move on to look at the main products they offer and their main business lines.
3. We look at these business lines in a little more detail and see how they relate to one another.
4. Using this background, we look at the work flow involved in making a typical equity trade.

5. Finally, we cover the main equity products offered by the broker dealer division of an investment bank in detail. This is the main focus of this book.

Table of Contents:

1. Foreword — 1
2. In the Beginning…. The Basics of an Investment Bank — 6
   2.1. General Product Overview and Introduction — 6
   2.1.1. Fixed Income — 7
   2.1.1. Equity — 7
   2.1.1. The Buy Side and the Sell Side — 8
   2.2. General Business Segment Overview and Introduction — 8
   2.2.1. The Investment Banking Division — 9
   2.2.2. The Investment Management Division — 13
   2.2.1. The Broker Dealer Division — 15
   2.3. Internal Structure of an Investment Bank — 18
   2.3.1. The Front Office — 18
   2.3.1.1. The Front Office in the Investment Banking Division — 18
   2.3.1.2. The Front Office in the Investment Management Division — 19
   2.3.1.3. The Front Office in the Broker Dealer Division — 20
   2.3.2. The Middle Office — 21
   2.3.2.1. The Middle (and back) Office in the Investment Banking Division — 21
   2.3.2.2. The Middle Office in the Investment Management Division — 22
   2.3.2.3. The Middle Office in the Broker Dealer Division — 23
   2.3.3. The Back Office — 24
   2.3.3.1. The Back Office in the Investment Management Division — 24
   2.3.3.2. The Back Office in the Broker Dealer Division — 25

3. Broker Dealer Trade Lifecycle — 27
4. Single Stock Cash Equities — 31
    4.1. What are they? — 31
    4.2. Why do clients buy this product? — 45
5. Exchange Traded Funds — 48
    5.1. What are they? — 48
    5.2. Why do clients buy this product? — 50
6. Equity Research and Research Sales — 52
    6.1. What is it? — 52
    6.2. Why are clients interested in this? — 57
7. Program Trading — 59
    7.1. What is it? — 59
    7.2. Why do clients buy this product? — 61
8. Direct Market Access / Algorithm Trading — 64
    8.1. What is it? — 64
    8.2. Why do clients buy this product? — 66
9. Securities Lending — 68
    9.1. What is it? — 68
    9.2. Why do clients buy this product? — 72
10. Prime Brokerage Services — 74
    10.1. What is it? — 74
    10.2. Why do clients buy this product? — 78
11. Crossing — 79
    11.1. What is it? — 79
    11.2. Why do clients buy this product? — 82
12. Facilitation and Market Making — 84
    12.1. What is it? — 84
    12.2. Why do clients buy this product? — 86
13. Corporate Access — 89
    13.1. What is it? — 89
    13.2. Why are clients interested in this? — 91
14. Equity Options — 93
    14.1. What are they? — 93
    14.2. Why do clients buy this product? — 106

- 15. Structured Derivatives — 109
  - 15.1. What are they? — 109
  - 15.2. Why do clients buy this product? — 113
- 16. Delta One — 115
  - 16.1. What is it? — 115
  - 16.2. Why do clients buy this product? — 120
- 17. Equity Futures and Forwards — 122
  - 17.1. What are they? — 122
  - 17.2. Why do clients buy this product? — 132
- 18. Equity Swaps — 134
  - 18.1. What are they? — 134
  - 18.2. Why do clients buy this product? — 138
- 19. Warrants — 140
  - 19.1. What are they? — 140
  - 19.2. Why do clients buy this product? — 145
- 20. Convertible Bonds — 146
  - 20.1. What are they? — 146
  - 20.2. Why do clients buy this product? — 150
- 21. Proprietary Trading — 152
  - 21.1. What is it? — 152
- 22. Conclusion — 156

Two

In the Beginning…. The Basics of an Investment Bank

2.1. General Product Overview and Introduction

Basically, an investment bank is not a bank as in a place to put money in the form of deposits, in fact it is quite the opposite. At its core, an investment bank is a place to "get" money. Historically, investment banks started off helping governments raise money to cover expenses; usually this money was raised to pay for wars. While governments are still an important client for investment banks, individual companies and corporations are now more common clients. Regardless, both governments and corporations are institutions and are thus known as "institutional clients". The term "institutional equity" refers to equity products developed for and sold to institutional clients. This is what this book will focus on.

An investment bank assists institutional clients in raising capital or "money". Of course these clients can also go to a regular bank to get a loan just like you or I can, but a bank loan is just not a flexible and cheap enough way to "get" money. An investment bank provides clients more flexibility in terms of how the capital can be raised and also makes it easier to raise larger sums of capital than a simple bank loan can provide.

Investment banks are all about providing access to capital; bringing together those who want to raise capital with those who have capital. There are two main product groups that they offer that allow clients to do this.

2.1.1. Fixed Income

One way an investment bank offers clients the ability to raise money is by assisting them in issuing bonds. A bond is simply a promise to repay a sum of money at a certain future point in time and until that time the borrower will pay a little sum of money known as "interest" for the privilege of borrowing the money from the lender. The investment bank assists clients who want to issue bonds by basically acting as a sales agent and selling them to the general investing public on behalf of the client. The proceeds of these bond sales are then given to the client who then uses the capital raised to invest back into their business.

Bonds were the first product that the investment banks dealt with when they first started helping governments raise money to pay for wars. They are still an important product to this day as both governments and corporations issue them. The bond product is usually referred to as "fixed income" because the interest payments made by the borrower are made in fixed amounts on fixed days.

2.1.1. Equity

The other major product that investment banks offer clients to assist them in raising capital is known as "equity". Equity is also known by other names such as "stock" or "shares" but basically equity is the issuance of ownership rights in a corporation and these make the investor a part owner in the company and therefore entitled to any profits in the company should there be any. The investment bank assists clients in issuing shares and selling them to the investing public on behalf of the clients. The clients then use this capital to invest in their businesses.

2.1.1. The Buy Side and the Sell Side

Before we go on to look at the structure of an investment bank in detail, there are two key terms that you will encounter in the world of investment banking; "the buy side" and "the sell side". The sell side refers to the investment banks that are selling investment products and services like the equities and bonds we mentioned.

The buy side consists of a variety of institutions such as; asset management firms, hedge funds, investment management firms, pension funds, charities, governments, private equity funds, sovereign wealth funds, educational institutions and other such institutions. These institutions are the investors aiming to earn a return on the capital that they invest in the bonds and stocks sold by the investment bank. These clients will place orders for products and services from the investment bank with this aim in mind. It is important to note that while individual investors participate in the markets, the term "buy side" is not applied to them, "the buy side" refers institutional clients and not individuals. For individual investors, the term "retail" is used instead.

• • •

2.2. General Business Segment Overview and Introduction

Investment banking has changed a lot over the years and has added a lot more services and products to meet the ever growing needs of its clients since the days when they first raised money for governments. Now there are generally three main product segments most investment banks offer, especially the large and dominant players within the industry. These business segments are;

1. Investment banking
2. Investment management
3. Broker / dealer (which is the focus of this book)

It is important to note that not all investment banks are structured exactly the same way and some may or may not have these divisions and others may have other divisions that they consider separate entities such as; research, wealth management or real estate. However, we want to focus on these three as they are they are the most common and they will serve to give you an overall picture of the industry.

2.2.1. The Investment Banking Division

The original purpose of an investment bank, as noted earlier, is to help clients raise capital in a process known as "underwriting". A corporation or government will approach an investment bank with the desire to raise capital in either the form of an equity issue (only corporations can offer ownership rights in the form of stock, governments are not involved in this) or a bond issue (available to both corporations and governments). The process of underwriting is very similar for the two product types. The investment banking division works with the client to determine the details of the security they want to create and provides guidance and advice to the client on what the market would be interested in buying and for how much.

Once all the details for the issue have been worked out, the investment banking division will help the client create the security which is known as "issuing". Then the investment bank through its broker dealer division -which we will cover in more detail soon- will act as a sales agent for the securities (either bonds or equity) issued by the client using its knowledge and experience in the market and its distribution channels to sell the product to the public and market participants such as the "the buy side" firms we mentioned earlier. The investment bank will makes money from the sales of these securities by selling them for a certain price and giving a discounted amount back to the issuing client. Perhaps the securities will be sold to the public for $10 per security and the issuing client will receive $9 and the investment bank will keep $1. This spread on the price they pay to the client and what they sell it to the public for is known as the "underwriting spread" and this is how the investment bank makes a profit when issuing securities. The investment bank pays the cash up front to the issuer and then turns around and sells the securities to the public in what is known as a public offering (PO). You may have heard this term, especially the term IPO, which is often mentioned in the financial media. A PO (public offering) or an IPO (initial public offering) refers to the selling of the shares or bonds. A public offering is simply the issuing of additional securities on top of securities that the client has already issued in the past. Initial public offerings are exactly that, the first time that the client has ever issued securities to the public. The investment banking division is considered part of the "sell side" since they are involved in the creation of securities and the sale of them to the investing public.

When the investment bank helps clients issue and sell securities to the investing public it takes on a lot of risk since it pays the client issuing the securities first then tries to sell the securities to the public. What happens if they cannot sell them all? What happens if there is no demand for the securities from the investing public? The investment bank could lose a lot of money if it agrees to pay the issuing client up front and then not be able to sell the securities in the PO or IPO. In the initial stages of the issuing process, the investment bank will first assess if there is enough demand in the market and work with the issuing client regarding the amount of capital that they can expect to raise.

Even with all this preparation, this is still a lot of risk for one investment bank to take on alone. In order to reduce risk and increase the opportunity to sell the securities, the investment bank will partner up with other investment banks increasing the total reach of their potential sales network and spreading the risk between them. These groups of investment banks form what is known as a "syndicate" and will work with the issuing client to sell the securities. This brings benefits to all parties; the issuing client has gained access to a bigger sales network and the investment bank has been able to share the risk amongst other investment banks and also increase sales through the bigger network.

In addition to POs and IPOs, the investment banking division will also offer services concerning mergers and acquisitions. Clients will come to an investment bank to discuss strategies around expanding their business. Usually a client is looking to purchase another company or perhaps one part of the business of another company. They may be looking for businesses that are complimentary to their own, or perhaps they are looking to get into a new type of business that might not exactly be related to their core business. The clients will rely on the investment bank's knowledge of the market and the individual companies within it to help them come up with ideas. The investment bank will employ a team of analysts who are specialists in a certain sector of the economy and or a certain group of companies within a sector. These analysts will provide insight and advice to the company looking to do a potential acquisition. Analysts will offer ideas to clients around possible target companies, advising how the potential targets might integrate with the client's existing business, advising how much the target company is worth and how much the client should offer for it. Finally, should the client decide to pursue the transaction, the investment bank will assist with the financing arrangements needed to make the purchase.

Conversely, the company being acquired will also hire an investment bank to provide advice to it as they will be seeking to get the best price for their shareholders from any offers made, or perhaps they might try to defend themselves from a hostile takeover by the acquirer. When the investment bank advises target companies this is known as a "sell side engagement" as the company being acquired is "selling" itself. When the investment bank advises the acquiring company this is known as a "buy side assignment".

In addition, the investment bankers will come up with ideas on how the clients can improve their business by suggesting possible mergers or acquisitions that they feel will complement their client's business strategy. Indeed, the "pitching" of ideas like this to clients is a large part of the sales activity the investment banking division is involved in.

It is important to note that most of the work within the investment banking section is considered secret and non public information as it reflects upcoming and possible future events such as POs and IPOs that if known in advance could influence prices in the markets. In order to prevent this, the investment banking division, the investment management division, and the broker dealer division are separated by what are known as "Chinese Walls". This is a barrier designed to prevent disclosure of information from those in the investment banking division who know information that can influence investment decisions from those in the investment management and broker dealer divisions who make investment decisions and carry them out. Investment banking is not allowed to disclose details on what POs and IPOs they are working on nor what companies have come to them for advice on mergers or acquisitions as this creates a conflict of interest. The sharing of such details would give unfair or "insider knowledge" to employees in the other divisions. This is what insider trading is all about; having possession of information that is not publically known or should not be publically known and using that advantage to make money. There have been numerous cases of this happening all throughout the history of investment banking. Sometimes employees who knew details on an upcoming deal would use this knowledge to make a personal profit in the markets.

In other cases, they would offer up this information to clients in order to build a better relationship with them. Regardless, the use of insider information to make a personal profit or to pass on to clients is forbidden by law.

2.2.2. The Investment Management Division

The investment management division of an investment bank is tasked with helping clients manage their investment capital in order to help them meet their goals. The client base is a little wider than that of the investment banking division including clients such as; pension funds, charities, trusts, private investors and educational institutions, in addition to the corporate clients and governments that might be shared with the investment banking division. Private investors will usually be handled by a separate group within the division specializing in dealing with high net worth clients and designing customized investment solutions for them. Regardless of the type of client, they are all looking for the same thing; to earn a return on their investment capital and will task the investment manager with achieving that goal.

Investment managers have access to a wide variety of assets and need to consider them all in their role. These are usually broken down into the 2 main classes we have already mentioned; equities and fixed income but investment managers will also deal with other assets like real estate, commodities and foreign exchange. The basic role of an investment manager is to provide a plan for how to allocate investment capital amongst the varying asset classes and then to suggest the specific securities to invest in within an asset class. Finally, the investment manager will monitor the performance of the investment and continue to manage the investment capital over time as things in the market develop and new opportunities to invest come along. Providing this service to clients usually takes one of two forms; advisory management or discretionary management.

The first is known as advisory management. This consists of providing advice on possible investments and investment strategies. The investment management division draws upon their in-depth knowledge of the market and the various companies participating in it to provide suggestions to clients in terms of asset allocation and investment planning (planning out the type of investments, and how much) as we mentioned. Based on these suggestions, the client will decide the course of action. Once the client has decided, the investment plan is put into action usually through a broker dealer with the broker dealer buying the products according to the plan. Finally, the investment manager will report the results back to the client.

The second type of service is known as discretionary management. This means that the investment manager provides more than just advice. Clients will expect the investment manager to actually control the investments giving them discretion to invest in whatever might be suitable. The client might establish a few guidelines around what their goals are and what can and cannot be invested in, but other than that they surrender control of the investment capital to the investment manager and expect them to take care of it all from the planning of the investments, to the execution of the plan, to the reporting of results. This is a far more demanding task for the investment manager and consequently the fees charged to clients for this service are higher.

The investment management division of an investment bank is a "buy side" entity and thus it can be a client of the broker dealer division of the same investment bank. Even though they are part of the same overall company, the investment management division is an independent entity and thus it will deal with whichever broker dealers will provide for its needs and whichever provide the best service for the fees charged.

One final note we need to mention, even though we talk of the investment management division in terms of it being an overall part of an investment bank, the same general concepts covered above apply just as equally to independent investment management firms who are not part of any greater investment bank business structure and just specialize only in investment management.

2.2.1. The Broker Dealer Division

The term "broker dealer" is an often heard term in the world of investment banking. A broker dealer is a term used to describe the actions involved in the buying and selling of equities or bonds, the so called "trading" of securities on the major stock markets and bond markets of the world. This trading is consolidated within the broker dealer division of the investment bank.

"Brokering" is when the broker dealer takes buy and sell orders from clients for various investment products and helps the client complete these transactions which they could not normally do themselves. The broker dealer is licensed to deal with the exchanges or venues on which the products trade and they in turn offer clients access to these venues. The broker dealer is simply acting as an intermediary or agent between its clients and other participants in the market seeking to match up sell orders with buy orders so that transactions can be completed and vice versa. This is known as an "agency" business. The counterparty to the trade, as in who bought the security the client is selling, is not known to the client and indeed it does not matter. The broker dealer division is relied on to find those counterparties; ensure that the trades between participants occur, ensure that there are no issues with them, and finally ensure that everyone gets the products that they bought or the proceeds from the sale of a product in a timely manner.

Clients of the broker dealer consist of institutions such as; hedge funds, investment and asset managers, governments, charities, and educational institutions. Individuals can also be clients of a broker dealer but individuals and institutional clients are usually dealt with separately as their needs differ. While both types of client buy and sell securities, individual investors usually have less sophisticated requirements and usually buy smaller amounts of the investment products. Individual investors are usually handled in a separate brokerage division setup for them known as "retail". Institutional clients are usually more demanding and have greater investment knowledge so they are handled by the "wholesale" or "institutional" division within the broker dealer. Institutional investors have access to a far greater range of products and services than retail investors do and they will tend to trade in far greater volumes than retail investors do. Relationships with institutional clients are important as the clients can be a source of a lot of revenue for the broker dealer but in turn they expect high levels of service.

Regardless of the type of client, retail or institutional, the broker dealer earns money by charging clients for the services provided either by taking a small commission for each trade placed by clients, by charging a fee for the service, or by making money on the price difference (the spread) between how much they can buy a product for versus how much they can sell it to a client for. We will cover this in more detail as we look at each product the broker dealer sells to clients later on in this book.

Dealing is the other part of the broker dealer's business. Dealing is when the broker dealer uses its own capital to buy and sell shares with the hope that they can make a profit trading them. The dealer may buy or sell shares to its clients and or other market participants. The broker dealer part of the investment bank is heavily involved in the PO and IPO process as a "market maker". They buy the securities offered in the PO / IPO (these would have been created by the investment banking division) using its own capital. Then the broker dealer division acting as a dealer will sell these securities to others in the market including the investment management division. It is in the broker dealer division where the ties to the other two divisions are most evident; taking products made in one to sell to another.

In addition to the market making activities as a dealer, the broker dealer may also trade with its own capital and will sometimes enter into transactions with clients taking one side of the transaction and the client taking the other. In this case the broker dealer is no longer simply an agent connecting two parties together to make a transaction but is in fact a principle part of the transaction. The terms; "principle business" and "agency business" are common terms used within the broker dealer to describe the difference between brokering and dealing.

Regardless of whether the broker dealer division is acting as a broker or a dealer, the division is usually split into two product groups, the same two products we looked at in the beginning; fixed income and equities. The fixed income group will sometimes also contain commodities and currencies in it depending on the structure of the broker dealer and the products they offer. In this sense, there can be a more diverse set of products in the broker dealer's fixed income division compared to the equity division.

Regardless of the product, fixed income or equities, the clients are really coming to the broker dealer division for two main reasons:

Content: providing the client with advice, research regarding investments, commentary and insight on the markets and of course recommendations on the products the broker dealer sells.

Execution: access to transact in financial products through the broker dealer and providing clients with sources of liquidity which allow them to buy or sell securities quickly without affecting the price too much and being able to sell securities converting them into cash quickly.

One final note we need to mention, even though we talk of the broker dealer division in terms of it being an overall part of an investment bank, the same general concepts covered above apply just as equally to independent broker dealer firms who are not part of any greater investment bank business structure.

• • •

2.3. Internal Structure of an Investment Bank

Now that we have an idea of what an investment bank is and how it is structured we need to go into a little more detail around how it functions internally. The three main business divisions of an investment bank are generally organized into three main areas known as "offices"; the front office, the middle office, and the back office. These terms are historic terms but they are still in use even though some investment banks have started to come up with newer and more "modern" terminology.

2.3.1. The Front Office

The front office is the start point for the entire investment bank. It is here that the firm makes sales to its clients. The term "front office" originates from the fact that it was physically the front part of the office that historically greeted clients as they entered the building. The front office has a similar role across the three main business divisions and that is to generate client business and bring in the revenues.

2.3.1.1. The Front Office in the Investment Banking Division

In the investment banking division the front office will respond to client inquiries regarding the raising of capital and any mergers and acquisitions that the client might be interested in. The front office staff are usually divided into teams that cover certain industry sectors such as telecoms, technology, health care amongst others. These groups are tasked with maintaining relationships with clients to handle their needs and also to market new ideas to them. Usually responses to client inquiries or suggestions for new ideas take the form of a "pitch book" that the team will work on and it will be used to "pitch" an idea to a client in the hopes that the client will agree to it and agree to do business with the bank. The pitch book concept is a core part of the work of winning business in the front office of the investment banking business division.

2.3.1.2. *The Front Office in the Investment Management Division*

In the investment management division the front office is, as you might have guessed, all about sales and client relationships. Fund managers deal directly with their clients such as pension funds, endowments, trust or charities etc and gather up their needs and desires in terms of what they expect from their portfolios of assets. They are also there to help educate clients on what is possible and realistic in the current investing environment given current economic, political and social conditions.

The fund managers are also expected to "pitch" new ideas and solutions to clients as well and this will take the form of a detailed pitch book just like in the investment banking division. The contents will be centered on how the portfolio will be structured, the investment strategies to be used, asset allocation, the actual products to be invested in, and the projected rate of return.

The front office staff are responsible for the management of the portfolios and this may vary depending on the level of discretion the client has given as we noted before. The fund managers will implement and decide on the asset allocation and the general strategy of the portfolio in consultation with the client and of course being wary of regulatory issues and concerns.

Traders are also an integral part of the front office in the investment management division. They will take the investment decisions of the fund managers and execute the buy and sell orders by sending them to the broker dealers with whom they have relationships, including sending orders over to the broker dealer division of the same investment bank in addition to other broker dealers on the "street". The traders will attempt to get the best prices that they can for the fund manager and by extension for the clients of the portfolios the investment manager manages. Having access and relationships with a large variety of broker dealers allows for this as certain broker dealers might know certain segments of the market better and thus be more specialized in particular types of products or services.

2.3.1.3. The Front Office in the Broker Dealer Division

In the broker dealer division, the front office is basically the sales office tasked with capturing client's orders and executing them. The majority of those working within the front office are tasked with sales and the focus is on selling products and services to clients. They are responsible for building relationships with the clients and learning what each client needs and how to fulfill that need as a part of being an effective sales force. In addition, they are expected to anticipate client needs and be proactive in selling products and services that they feel their clients would be interested in. Each sales person is usually assigned a group of clients to cover based on their product specialty. We will look at this in more detail as we get into the products, how they are sold and who sells them.

While it is common across all the three divisions for the main focus to be on sales, there is also a strong support element present in the front office. IT support is ever present ensuring the systems are operating properly and attending to any IT related issues that would impact the sales organization such as system outages. IT support while tasked with supporting the front office is not usually considered an "official" part of the front office in terms of organization but it is important to mention their role in keeping the business running.

The second support element is known as sales support. They are tasked with a variety of tasks usually related to tracking what products the clients buy and the activities of the sales people in terms of revenues they bring in. They are also involved in other sales support activities with the sales staff and support management in the day to day running of the business.

2.3.2. The Middle Office

The middle office provides many essential services that support the client's buying and selling of the services sold by investment bank's front office sales force. They are the ones to actually process the transactions between the client and the investment bank and ensure that there are no issues.

2.3.2.1. The Middle (and back) Office in the Investment Banking Division

In the investment banking division, the difference between the middle and back office is a little more "blurry" compared to the investment management and broker dealer divisions. Indeed the terms "middle office" and "back office" are not used the same as in the other two divisions. We will treat them here as one piece to simplify things. In the investment banking division "the middle-back office" is more concerned with compliance and regulatory controls. The big concern in investment banking is secrecy and protecting the confidential deals that clients are planning on doing. Ensuring that these controls are in place and are being followed is a big part of the function. In addition, since a lot of the work is contractually based and the contracts will vary from deal to deal, the legal department is called upon heavily to support the sales activities in the front office.

This function would be considered to be a part of the "middle-back office".

Research may be treated as a "middle-back" function in the investment banking division depending on how client facing they are. The research teams are relied on to provide research that makes up the contents of the sales pitches to clients in the form of the pitch book as noted. The research teams will analyze the situation and provide industry specific details on the situation in the market as well as looking at the macro conditions. They will also analyze trends, strengths and weaknesses and look at valuation scenarios.

Finally, the finance and risk departments will be heavily relied on during deals as there are significant risks that need to be considered when the firm is involved in raising capital for its clients. The underwriting of securities needs to be carefully monitored during this process.

2.3.2.2. The Middle Office in the Investment Management Division

In the investment management division, the middle office is tasked with managing and controlling the trades made by the front office traders. A large part of this revolves around the reconciliation of the trades they made with the broker dealers. The middle office will receive trade confirmations on a daily basis from the broker dealers and will ensure that there are no issues with the trades and provide settlement booking details to the broker dealers as well as dealing with the custodian of the securities to make sure that everything is correct in terms of positions held at the end of the trading day. They will also handle corporate actions like stock dividends and stock splits should they occur during the time that the investment manager holds the securities in their portfolios.

In some investment management divisions, the middle office may also contain the IT, audit, internal control, risk management, legal and compliance and finance functions. In others, these may be considered back office roles. Regardless, these functions provide support for the division ensuring that the law is being complied with, and that the various risks inherent in the business are properly managed.

2.3.2.3. The Middle Office in the Broker Dealer Division

The middle office in a broker dealer is similar to that of the investment management division as both deal with securities trading and trade flows. The middle office will help the clients like investment managers reconcile the trades made during the day and ensure that there are no issues like trade breaks when trade details do not match. In this regard, they will face off directly with middle office counterparts at their clients like that of the investment manager above. They will often have to deal with the internal front office staff in confirming details of any trades that might be in question as the front office sales staff are responsible for taking the orders.

Middle office staff will receive the allocation instructions from clients. These instructions instruct the broker dealer what to do with the shares and how they should be allocated amongst any sub accounts that the client might have. From time to time, new accounts or new sub accounts might be needed should the client request and the middle office will take care of setting these up as well. Once the trades are allocated the middle office will deal with the custodian whom is responsible for the exchange of cash for the securities bought or sold. Once this is complete, the trade will move on the settlement process which is covered by the back office.

The middle office will be tasked with client reporting activities. They will provide a confirmation for all the trades made to the client reporting the prices and amounts bought and sold. They usually face off to the middle office equivalents at their clients -like those of the investment manager as mentioned above- in resolving any issues.

IT, audit, internal control, risk management, legal and compliance, and finance functions may be included within the middle office just like with the investment management division. The roles carried out by these functions are much the same as those in investment managers.

2.3.3. The Back Office

The back office is mainly concerned with the movement of the securities and ensuring that every party involved has gotten the securities they expect and that they have paid for them or have been paid for them.

2.3.3.1. The Back Office in the Investment Management Division

The back office in the investment manager is mainly concerned with administering the portfolios and ensuring that the trades made with the broker dealers are correctly handled.

When it comes to administering the portfolios, there is a large accounting function which makes sure that everything is properly recorded and correct. Valuation exercises for the individual securities within portfolios are checked and calculated and these are summed up to reflect the net asset value of the portfolio as a whole. This is prepared for distribution to the investment manager's end clients. This function will also handle the fees and commissions charged to clients ensuring that they are properly collected and that documentation on those fees are prepared for the clients.

The back office will also deal with handling any regulatory and compliance issues and ensuring that any reporting or registration needs for the portfolios they manage are handled with the appropriate authorities in each legal jurisdiction.

The other major part of the role will be handling the clearing and settlement of trades with the broker dealers. We will cover this in more detail in the broker dealer section below as it is quite similar.

2.3.3.2. The Back Office in the Broker Dealer Division

In the broker dealer, the back office will be involved primarily in the settlement and clearing of trades. Clearing is all about confirming the differing claims between financial institutions. The claims refer to the buying and selling of securities. As the broker dealers buy and sell for their clients they need to exchange securities for cash and vice versa. Clearing is all about matching up and confirming these claims of cash for securities. The back office will deal with a clearing house which acts as an intermediary between buyers and sellers in the market ensuring that all the trades are actually completed. Clearing houses are entities set up by and jointly owned by market participants such as broker dealers to act as a central processing hub for all the trades made in the market by all the participants. It is much easier for all the parties to the trade to deal with one central hub as opposed to sending money and securities back and forth amongst potentially thousands of counterparties for millions of individual trades. The central role they play is to ensure that the trade can be completed by acting as the counterparty to all trades. They will take the role as a buyer or seller for any trade that has an issue allowing the trade to be completed successfully while the issues are resolved in the meantime. Thus, the broker dealer is expected to keep some collateral with the clearing house to help facilitate this process and the back office will be involved with the management of this as well.

As trades are executed, the details are recorded and confirmations are sent between all the parties involved. These trades are then netted out by the clearing house meaning that the buy and sell differences are compared and the difference between them becomes the amounts that need to finally be exchanged between the broker dealers. The netting process reduces the number of transactions that need to be considered to a more manageable amount. Once all these records are confirmed and "cleared up", the clearing house will alert the back office of the broker dealers as to what they need to deliver to complete the trades.

The back office also handles the settlement process. Settlement is the actual movement of money and securities between the counterparties involved in the trade. The clearing house will be involved in this process as well. The back office will engage in the movement of cash and securities with the clearing house based on what was netted out. Doing this completes the trade as each party has fulfilled their part of the contract as either buyer or seller. Should the settlement process fail for some reason, the back office staff will be tasked with resolving these issues working with the clients helping to ensure that the trades settle correctly and that there are not any broken trades that do not match up remaining.

The back office is also involved in the monitoring of client accounts to ensure that compliance regulations are adhered to. Margin considerations on the client's accounts are also checked and reconciled as needed. Any accounting and finance issues are also handled by the back office as well.

Three

Broker Dealer Trade Lifecycle

Now that we have covered the overall structure of the investment bank, its business divisions and its structure and functions within them, let's now turn to focus on the broker dealer's trading of equities.

In this section we will map the functions covered in the previous section to the life cycle of a typical equity trade. This will give you a clearer picture of who is involved and what roles they take.

Process Flow:	Who Handles it:	Actions Performed:	Key Interactions:
Pre Trade	Front Office	**General Market Conditions:** The sales staff and traders at the broker dealer will discuss the general market conditions with the clients and provide them with "color" on what is happening in the markets. The goals here are to try to find out what the client is looking for and also capture the client's interest that will hopefully lead to orders to trade.	Fund managers at the client
Pre Trade	Front Office	**Research:** The sales staff work closely with the research analysts and will seek out specific research that they feel their clients would be interested in. They will present these research reports to the clients to build their interest and seek to solicit orders from the client. This is known as research sales.	Fund managers at the client. Internal research analysts.
Pre Trade	Front Office	**Trading Ideas:** The sales staff and traders are expected to come up with specific trading ideas that meet client needs. These are then offered to clients and orders are solicited from the clients.	Fund managers at the client Internal sales staff and research analysts.
Trade	Front Office	**Order Capture:** During the pre trade process, the sales staff pitches trade ideas to the clients. Traders at the client will send in orders as instructed by their portfolio manager to traders at the broker dealer. Traders at the broker dealer accept these orders (or reject them if there are any issues). These orders will include the instructions as to how the clients want the trades to be carried out. The traders at the broker dealer and the buy side client will be in contact throughout the rest of the trade process.	Traders at the client
Trade	Front Office	**Order Management:** The traders manage the captured orders in an order management system (OMS). The OMS allows the traders to see which orders they have received from the client and see what the current status of the order is.	Traders at the client

INSTITUTIONAL EQUITIES AND THE BROKER DEALER

Process Flow:	Who Handles it:	Actions Performed:	Key Interactions:
Trade	Front Office	**Order Routing:** Orders are routed to various venues for execution. Traders will do this based on what they feel will best achieve the results that the client is looking for. Orders can be routed for manual execution or to an algorithm for execution without human intervention. Orders can also be routed to various exchanges, dark pools, crossing networks and other places where buyers and sellers come together.	Exchanges and execution venues
Trade	Front Office	**Execution:** This is the heart of the entire business as this is where the client's orders get filled and where the investment bank collects its commissions. Traders using the instructions picked up when the order was captured will attempt to fill the orders. Clients would have specified the prices that they are willing to receive and they would have provided instructions as to how the order is to be "worked". The trader can manually split the order up buying or selling little pieces of it at a time based on price movements in the market. This is called "working an order". The goal is to achieve the best price for the client. Orders can also be routed to automatic algorithms for execution. These algorithms will also attempt to obtain the best prices for clients just like a human trader would.	Exchanges and execution venues
Post Trade Processing	Middle Office	**Allocation:** Clients will provide instructions on how they want the executed order to be allocated amongst the various portfolios that they have. These may come in from the fund manager or from the middle office at the client. The middle office at the broker dealer will deal with the client to ensure that the allocation process is dealt with correctly, any issues are resolved and the results are communicated to the client.	Middle office staff at the client
Post Trade Processing	Middle Office	**Confirmation:** The middle office will send out a confirmation to the clients at the end of the day letting the client know all the orders received and what parts of the orders were filled and not filled. Sometimes an order may not be filled if the price did not meet what the client wanted.	Middle office staff at the client
Post Trade Processing	Middle Office	**Reconciliation:** The middle office will ensure that the trades are matched up with the clients and that all expected trades have been acknowledged by the clients. All the details of the trades must match up including the side (meaning buy or sell in this case), price, quantity and of course the security that was bought or sold. The confirmations that go out to clients play a large role in this as they are one of the ways that issues can be detected. Should issues appear, the middle office will work with the clients to resolve broken trades.	Middle office staff at the client

Process Flow:	Who Handles it:	Actions Performed:	Key Interactions:
Clearance	Back Office	**Trade Matching:** The back office will deal with the clearing house which acts as the counterparty between each of the parties to the transaction; the buyer and the seller. The trades will be matched up with the clearing house and the back offices of the buying and selling counterparties and the broker dealer as the agent of one of the counterparties will be involved. Any trades with issues or "breaks" will be dealt with at the same time.	Clearing house, back office staff at the client
Clearance	Back Office	**Netting:** The back office will work with the clearing house to net out the trades with the buy and sell differences compared and the difference between them becoming the amounts that need to finally be exchanged.	Clearing house
Settlement	Back Office	**Securities Transfer:** The back office will be involved with the transfer of securities to the clearing house. The clearing house will hold the securities in what is called "street name" (the name of the broker dealer). This means that the broker dealer actually holds the security on behalf of the client making it easy to move securities between broker dealers as opposed to between millions of individuals and institutions who are the end clients of the broker dealers. The back office staff at the broker dealer will also have to ensure that their internal records of client securities are updated as well.	Clearing house
Settlement	Back Office	**Cash Transfer:** The back office will deal with the clearing house and arrange for the transfer or receipt of funds based on the overall netted out results of that day's trading activity. Broker dealers that have net credit at the end of the day will receive funds and brokers with net debits will have to send funds. The back office will also ensure that all the client accounts within their firm are correctly debited and or credited. Once this is complete, the trades are considered settled and the contractual obligations of each party to the trade completed. In addition, the back office will be involved with resolving any issues with any trades that are still broken.	Clearing house

While the above process flow is for an equities trade, the same general flow applies to the other equity products as well with some small differences of course. Ok, so then what are all these other equity products we have been talking about? What is the broker dealer selling and how are they making money on them?

Four

Single Stock Cash Equities

4.1. What are they?

Single stock cash equities are the first product that we will cover in this book as they are the fundamental equity product for the broker dealer.

At their core stocks or shares represent a unit of ownership in the business which is known as equity. As owners of the business, stock holders are entitled to receive the earnings of the company if any, and have a say in how the company is run. If the company makes any earnings this will sometimes be distributed to the owners in the form of a dividend. A dividend is a small payment of earnings given out to the owners on a per share basis. The more shares an owner owns the more of the profit they will receive. Companies also allow their shareholders the right to vote on key issues that affect the company. Shareholders will be able to vote on the management and "elect" them to run the company as well as vote on major issues that affect corporate policy and issues that might ultimately impact the dividends that the owners of the company receive. The amount of dividends and voting rights available to shareholders will vary between companies and will also change over time.

As an owner of the company, there is the possibility of losing all your investment in the company should the company go bankrupt. In the event of a bankruptcy, those who lent money to the company in the form of bonds or bank loans get paid first. If there is any money left over the owners of the firm will receive that back based on a per share basis. Bankruptcy or failure of the business is one of the risks that all shareholders must face.

Shares come in two basic forms; the preferred share and the common share. Preferred shares are a special class of shares that are really a hybrid instrument that has some features of a bond and has some features of an equity share. Preferred shares have no voting rights and in that sense are similar to bonds which also have no voting rights. In the event of a bankruptcy, the preferred shares rank ahead of the common shares when it comes time to break up the company. However, they rank behind bond holders or holders of debt. Finally, preferred shares often tend to be callable which means that the issuing company can call them back and redeem them giving you the investor the capital in return. This call price is usually set at the time the preferred stock is created and the time limit for this call feature is usually set as well allowing the company the discretion to call the shares back anytime up until the time limit.

Preferred shares are entitled to dividends and in this regard they function as an equity share. In fact have greater claim to dividends than do common shares. Preferred shares tend to have more clearly defined dividends in which a fixed amount of dividend is declared and payable on the preferred share. Dividends issued by the company are distributed first to the preferred shares and then to the common stock which means that there are times that there might not be enough of a dividend to pay the common shareholders. However, in times of financial distress, a company can forgo a dividend even on preferred shares, thus the income is not always regular like is expected with a bond. Some preferred shares have provisions that allow the investor to receive missed dividends at a later date once the company is able to pay dividends again, something common shares do not have.

There are various types of preferred shares available and these will differ depending on the company. Some may offer voting rights but only in exceptional cases and others may have differing rules around how the dividends are paid compared to the common stock. Sometimes there are options available to convert preferred shares to common stock under certain conditions.

Common shares on the other hand, are the ones that most people will buy and sell on the stock markets of the world. Holders of common stock have rights to participate in voting and are entitled to dividends as owners of the business. However, the payment of a dividend on common shares is far more varied and at the discretion of the board of directors of the company and if there is no dividend payment, well too bad as there is no recourse to getting a dividend payment later to make up for the one missed as there is with preferred shares. Common shares tend to be more standardized and do not have the options and variations that are seen in preferred shares. Finally, the biggest and most important difference is that common shares also tend to increase in value while preferred shares do not. The reason for this is that preferred shares tend to be callable and the call price is known so no one is going to buy the preferred share at a price above the call price when the company could call back the shares anytime and only pay the lower call price. Now, a company can buy back common shares as well and this does happen, but the difference is that the company has to buy back the common shares in the market at the market prices at that time.

Cash equities encompass both preferred and common shares and they are simply bought with and sold for cash. They are a cash instrument and this is where the term "cash equity" comes from. Clients will come to the broker dealer to have them execute the buys and sells for them with the broker acting as an agent for the client. Cash equities as a product are a product offering in and of themselves but, are also the basis for a lot of the other equity product offerings that we will cover in this book.

A cash equity order represents a single order to buy or sell a single security. Clients will purchase these with cash and receive cash in return when they sell them. They are also known as single stock cash equities as they are composed of one order for a single stock at a time. Single stock cash equities are traded on stock exchanges around the world by participants both large and small, ranging from the institutional clients the broker dealer will deal with to the general public who are known as retail clients. The prices of shares of the individual companies in the stock market are determined by the forces of supply and demand with market participants making offers on how much of a certain stock they are willing to buy or sell and at what price. If a particular stock is in high demand, market participants will be willing to pay more for it. The prices that the participants are willing to pay are known as "the bid price". If a particular stock is in high supply; as in lots of participants wanting to sell it, then the price will fall as sellers will lower the price to make it more attractive until some other participant buys it. The prices that sellers are offering to buy at is known as "the ask price" or how much a participant is "asking" someone to pay for the stock.

So we know that supply and demand determine the overall price but what things are influencing the participants as to how much they are willing to pay for an individual stock? In reality there are a wide variety of things that influence a person; far too many to cover here but we will cover some of the main ones which break down into three types, fundamental factors, technical factors and finally market sentiment.

The most important of the three types are the fundamental factors. This involves looking at the company and seeing what makes it tick. Market participants look at the fundamental, or basic factors, that affect the company. This can include external factors such as the economy as a whole and the industry that the company is in and it will also include internal factors such as looking at financial data from within the company to determine its financial health. After all, no one wants to own a company that does not make any money and the fundamental reason for a firm to exist is to make money. A company that earns money is one that is desirable to investors and thus it is the earnings of the company that are the single most important fundamental factor in determining what market participants are willing to pay for a share in a company. A company with a record of solid and ever increasing earnings is generally seen as desirable and one with a history of volatile earnings or declining earnings is not. How much the company earns now and how much it is expected to earn in the future influence how much people are willing to pay for the stock or how much they are willing to sell the stock for.

One of the most looked at ratios is the price earnings ratio -or the PE ratio- and you would probably have come across this in the financial news media. This is directly tied to the concept of earnings. It is a simple ratio which takes the current market price per share and divides it by the earnings over the last 12 months. You can look at it as the amount that market participants are willing to pay for the earnings of the firm. A PE ratio of 10 means that market participants are willing to pay $10 for every $1 of earnings a firm makes thus a higher PE ratio means that people are willing to pay more for the same amount of earnings. How can this make sense? Why would you pay more for $1 of earnings for one company compared to another? Well a high PE ratio means that people expect that the company will have higher earnings in the future and thus make a greater profit in the future. Greater future earnings will equal a greater future stock price and it is best to buy now with the anticipation of selling at a higher price later; "buy low and sell high" as the saying goes.

Technical factors also play a part in how market participants determine how much they are willing to buy or sell and at what price. The technical factors most looked at are price and volume. There is not much consideration of fundamental factors like earnings; instead technical analysis tries to find patterns in the chaos of data. This can be found in the charts that plot the data used in technical analysis. You may have heard some of the following terms in the financial media; "moving averages", "head and shoulders", "lines of support", "lines of resistance", "double bottom". All these are part of technical analysis and these are looked at to determine the price movement in the near future. If market participants feel it will move up, then they will usually buy with the hope to sell at a higher price later. If they feel it will fall, then they will sell what they have or short sell the stock to make a profit.

Finally there is market sentiment, unlike fundamental or technical factors this is not based as much on data (although data still plays a role and indeed efforts are underway to capture this more in a way that it can be analyzed as data) but instead represents how the various market participants in general "feel" about a stock. Even after all the data analysis found in fundamental and technical analysis, there is still never a 100% certainty that a stock price will move up or down. Indeed, it is possible to find stocks with strong earnings fundamentals that should have an increasing stock price but end up having the opposite. This does not seem to make logical sense yet it happens all the time and this may be due to market sentiment. It looks at the psychology of the market participants. Factors such as recent new stories, general feelings and even rumours about a stock form a part of what market sentiment is all about. Market sentiment can be based on logical or even illogical feelings about a stock but it does serve to affect the prices of stocks.

So then how do the market participants interact with the single stock cash equity and buy and sell them? There are three main types of order that can be made with the broker dealer for a cash equity; you either buy them or sell what you already own or you can short sell them. Buying and selling are pretty straight forward but let's quickly look at an example of how a client purchases or sells them through a broker dealer and how the broker dealer charges a client for the service of acting as an agent.

If a client wants to buy shares, they would have to pay the amount equal to the number of shares multiplied by the purchase price per share. In addition to this, the broker dealer will charge a commission fee. This is the fundamental way that the broker dealer charges clients for its services. This is true for the single stock cash equity we will cover in this section as well as on most of the other products we will cover in this book. Commissions taken on the value of the financial transaction made are the single most important way the broker dealer charges clients for its services.

Commissions are measured in basis points. Basis points are equal to one hundredth of a percentage point and are the industry standard for measuring commissions in addition to other things. For example, the client wants to buy 100 shares of ABC Incorporated for $50.00 thus the client would need to pay $5,000 to the broker dealer. The broker dealer tells the client that the fee in this case will be 15 basis points or 0.0015 which means: $5,000 * 0.0015 = $7.5 so the total cost to the client is $5,007.50. The client will pay this amount to the broker dealer who would in turn settle the transaction and receive 100 shares of ABC Incorporated to put in the client's account. The client does not know from whom they bought the shares (the counterparty to the transaction) and the broker dealer will probably not know either. The market does not list up the names of the sellers (and buyers) only the quantities and the prices people want to buy or sell at.

For a sell, the same basic concept applies; if the client were to sell shares they would receive the amount based on the number of shares multiplied by the sell price per share. For example, the client wants to sell 100 shares of XYZ Corporation for $50.00 thus the client would receive $5,000. Of course in this case the commission fee is also charged and let's assume it is also 15 basis points which as above is equal to $7.50 thus the client will receive $4,992.50. The broker dealer would take the 100 shares out of the client's account and deliver them to the buyer and receive the cash in exchange and deposit it in to the client's account thus settling the transaction.

But what about short selling, what is this third order type all about? Short selling is a special type of sell order. Basically with this order you can sell shares that you do not actually own. The broker dealer will lend the client shares through a service known as securities lending (which we will look at in detail later on). The client then takes these shares and immediately sells them on the market. Later on the client will buy back the shares at a lower price and repay those loaned shares back to the broker dealer. Just like with any loan the client will have to pay a fee for the use of the shares for the duration that they are used for.

Short selling works exactly the same as a sell order with the client paying commission measured as always in basis points because in the end it is still a trade and a financial transaction still takes place on the market. Likewise, when the client buys back the shares at a lower price in the future they will pay a commission on that buy order as well. There is no difference between a short sell and a regular sell order or the later buy order in terms of how commission works.

Short selling allows clients to make a profit on downward price movements in a single stock. However, short selling is not without risk as there is no limit to how high the price of the shares borrowed can go to meaning that the client could find themselves having to buy back the shares at a much higher price than they sold them for initially. Buying a stock the normal way -also known as "going long"- on the other hand limits the potential loss as shares prices can only ever go as low as $0.00. However, the flexibility to sell short is appealing to clients of the broker dealer looking to make short term gains on downward movements of stock prices.

There is one final point on short selling that is important to make and that is the concept of naked short selling; a practice that was banned in US markets in 2008 and in many other countries as well. A naked short sell is a sale of the shares that have not been borrowed in the first place. The idea is that one can sell the shares even without borrowing them and as long as they are able to deliver the shares to the buyer in time for settlement no one will know that the short sell was naked or not. What this means is that someone naked short selling a stock has to quickly buy the shares, usually within the same day, in order to deliver them to the buyer if they cannot buy the shares the trade will fail because they have no shares to deliver. A regular short sell has shares borrowed in advance ready to deliver to a buyer. This is the key difference between regular and naked short selling.

Once a client has decided on whether to buy or sell or short sell a stock, then the client will usually specify the type of buy or sell order that they want to conduct. The type of order is an instruction to the broker dealer that explains how the order is to be handled. The instructions a client will give to the broker dealer are based primarily on the price with certain time or quantity restraints added if the client feels like it.

Price based instructions fall into two types, market and limit orders. Market orders are simply orders that are placed on the market for buy or sale immediately at the best price available at that time. The price that the order will be executed at may vary from what the client placing the order thinks is the price that they will get. Prices in markets can move very quickly; the client might see the price move and think that the price is favourable and submit a market order to buy or sell it. However, in the time that the order takes to pass through to the exchange, even if just barely a second, the price could have moved outside of the expected price. A market order does not guarantee a price but it does guarantee that the order will be executed (filled) at the price in the market at that given time. It is important to note that a market order might contain different prices as it gets executed. For example, a client submits an order to buy for 500 shares or ABC Corporation as a market order. If the current market has 100 shares for sale at an ask price of $10.01 than the first 100 shares will be bought at $10.01. If the next 200 shares are available for $10.02 then they will be filled for $10.02 and so on until the order is filled. Each one of these transactions is called an execution and an order may have lots of executions within it. Each execution can have a different price in a market order depending on the situation in the market. Generally, the larger the market order; the more executions it will take to fill it and the greater the chance of different prices.

A limit order is an order where the price to buy or sell is set as a maximum limit. The client has control over the price and can set any limit that they wish however there is no guarantee that this order will be filled. If the price of the stock never falls within the limits then the order will never get executed. Of course if a better price is obtainable than that expressed as the limit then the broker dealer will attempt to get that price. For a buy order, the price has to be lower than or equal to the limit with the limit equaling a price ceiling that will not be crossed. For a sell order, the price has to be higher than or equal to the limit with limit equaling a price floor.

Just like with a market order, there may be various executions made at various quantities and prices but the prices will always be within the limit.

There is another order type known as a stop order. It appears to be similar to a limit order but it functions a little differently. A stop order is an order to sell or buy the shares at the market price once a certain price has been obtained which acts as a trigger for the order. For example, a client has bought shares in the past at $8.00 a share. They want to get out of the position soon so they set a stop order for $9.00 which means that should the share price hit $9.00; it will be entered into the market and sold. The client can still make $1.00 a share profit in this case. However, once that stop price is reached, the shares will be sold and treated like a market order. $9.00 is not the price that the shares will be sold at and is not a limit price just the price that triggers the market order. The shares could still sell below $9.00 depending on price movements within the market especially if the market is rapidly declining. There is however a stop limit order which combines the features of a limit order with the trigger effect of a stop order. In the above example, $9.00 acts as the trigger for the order to sell as well as being the price at which it will be sold at. This way the client can control the price but like with a limit order there is no guarantee of execution. The price could hit $9.00 a share and rapidly fall below that meaning that there might not be any executions or a partial execution at best.

Time based instructions can also be added to market and limit orders. The most common is what is known as a "day order"; also called a "good for day order". All orders received from clients are treated by default as a day order unless otherwise specified. Day orders mean that the order is good for the entire trading day and remains open until the order is filled. If the order is not filled it or partially filled by the end of the trading day the unfilled part is cancelled. A "good 'til cancelled" order is one that remains open indefinitely until it is filled. It is not cancelled until the client specifically asks that it be cancelled. This allows a client to set a limit order with a price that they want and allow more time for the price to hit that limit as the price in a good for day order might not hit the limit price. The more time allowed for the order, the greater the chance it has to be executed and there is no need to reenter the order every day.

Finally, quantity based instructions can be used in conjunction with time and price instructions. Usually the quantity based instruction is combined with some type of time limit. An "immediate or cancel" order is an order that must be filled immediately or it will be considered cancelled. Filling this order also allows the order to be partially filled with whatever quantity is available in the market at that time. Basically it is an instruction asking the broker dealer to fill as much of the quantity as they can right now and cancel whatever they cannot fill. A "fill or kill" order is similar to the "immediate or cancel" order except that the entire quantity must be filled immediately and if not the order is cancelled. There are no partial fill quantities allowed. Finally, there is what is known as an "all or none" order. This order means that the entire order quantity must be filled at the price specified. However, if the order is not filled immediately it will not be cancelled right away. The "all or none" order can still remain open until another chance to fill it all at once appears.

We have covered the types of orders available and the instructions that clients can place on an order so now let's take this altogether and see how the process of actually buying or selling cash equities comes together at the broker dealer.

The sales traders start the day early in the morning usually around 6:00 or 6:30. They attend a morning meeting which discusses some of the news in the market as well as what has happened in other markets around the world over night. News and trading ideas are exchanged between the sales traders and others within the firm based on what they feel will happen in the upcoming day. After the meeting the sales traders prepare for the day.

During this preparation time one of the sales traders takes in the discussions at the meeting and comes up with a trading idea she knows one of her clients might like. She calls the portfolio manager at the client, a large pension fund, and pitches them the idea. She will discuss the reason why the trade idea is good bringing in some of the fundamental, technical or market sentiment factors as we mentioned before as a basis for her idea. The portfolio manager likes what he hears and agrees to buy the stock the sales trader recommended. The portfolio manager sends in a day order with a limit price through his trader at the pension fund.

The sales trader at the broker dealer accepts the client's order from the portfolio manager's trader with the price the portfolio manager assigned and she enters it into the order management system which contains all the buy and sell orders for her client as well as all the other clients. The sales trader can trade the order herself throughout the day or pass it to an execution trader to work the order for the client. The sales trader is focused on the actual sales aspect while the execution trader is focused on the actual trading. Regardless of which of them trades it, the goal is to try to get a better price than the client specified as the limit providing the client with the best execution which will in turn encourage the client to return to do business with the broker dealer.

In this case, the sales trader passes it to the execution trader for him to work on throughout the day with the price instructions the portfolio manager at the client gave. The execution trader will watch the order throughout the day and will "work the order" for the client at certain times when the prices look favourable and in accordance with the client's instructions and goals. The actual trading of the order is done in the execution management system which is connected to the exchange and allows the execution trader (or sales trader) to buy and sell single stocks and set the prices and quantities to be bought or sold, slicing the order up into pieces as needed. Each one of these pieces may become part of the execution of the order if it gets filled.

Luckily, the market conditions are good and the price is moving down so the execution trader is able to get a lower price for the order and by lunch has the order more than half filled. After lunch the price spikes above the limit so the execution trader is not able to trade the order any more. However, as luck would have it, the prices settle down below the limit again toward the end of the trading day and the execution trader gets a few good executions done and fills the entire order for the client.

It is important to note that sometimes either the execution or the sales trader may route the order to be executed in a different way. We will look at some of these different methods later on in the book as broker dealers offer more than just than just access to the stock market as a venue for execution.

After the trade is complete (filled) or as complete as it can be, at the end of the trading day the executions will move into the middle office systems where the middle office staff will send out the trade confirmations to the portfolio manager telling him what he has bought and at what prices. Also, the stock that was bought will be allocated or put into one or more of the portfolio manager's accounts depending on what accounts the portfolio manager was buying the stock for. Finally, in the back office, the staff will make sure that the shares bought are delivered into the accounts the portfolio manager specified during allocation and that the cash to pay for the shares is delivered to the counterparty.

• • •

4.2. Why do clients buy this product?

Since the single stock cash equity is so general, and forms the basis of most other products, a vast majority of the clients of a broker dealer would be involved in the purchase and sale of these instruments in one way or another.

Core Product / Ease of Understanding:

Cash equities as instruments are one of the core products in the investing world; the other being bonds as we mentioned in an earlier part of the book. Cash equities are the most basic of the products and given this position they make up a vast majority of client holdings and even if clients do not hold any cash equities in their portfolio in favour of other instruments, those other instruments are most certainly affected by the cash equities being traded throughout the stock markets of the world.

Equities are arguably the most common and most accessible instrument available to the general public. Most institutional clients at the end of the day are composed of clients in the general public who have given their funds to the institution to manage. Providing products to the general public based on equities is something that is easy to sell and thus the institutional client's holdings will consist of those same equities. This is further reinforced by the fact that performance in the investment management industry is based on the returns of overall stock markets which the public is also more familiar with thus again a lot of those same stocks end up in the portfolios of the institutions that are the clients of the broker dealer.

Dividends:

Buying shares grants the holder ownership in the firm and thus entitles them to receive a dividend from the company. The dividend represents a distribution of profit from the company whose shares the investor bought. Not all companies offer to pay dividends all the time and the payout rate on dividends can vary over time, never the less they are an important part of the overall return on the investment a shareholder would receive.

Voting Rights:

Being an owner of the shares in a company gives the holder a right to vote on major issues affecting the company and also vote on the appointment of the company's management. For institutional investors, this can be attractive depending on what their goals are. Certainly if an institution was attempting to take over another, buying out the majority of the voting rights in the target firm would be something that they would want to do. However, in practice the vast majority of the clients of a broker dealer rarely buy up large percentages of a company that would approach or exceed 50% of the voting rights. While large investors do buy up large amounts of shares, 5% or more is usually a cutoff point as most jurisdictions have rules around reporting who owns the largest parts of companies. In addition, investors usually want to diversify their holdings and thus there is less incentive to buy up huge portions of a firm. Nevertheless, holding large amounts of shares; even if not enough to take over a firm, does give the investor holding those shares enormous influence in a firm.

Long Term Investment Outlook:

Cash equities offer investors the opportunity to invest long term as there is no expiry date on shares as there might be with some other products we will cover. Holding the shares long term allows the investor to receive dividends over time and potentially benefit from any price increase in the form of capital appreciation over time. Of course capital appreciation is not guaranteed but the long term aspect of shares allows investors to hold them for as long as they wish.

The returns on equities that investors can expect have generally been higher than for other asset classes over the long term since the Second World War. Of course no one knows how long this can continue for and if it will always be the long term trend, but it has held up enough over the past 60-70 years to be a major reason to invest in equities.

Five

Exchange Traded Funds

5.1. What are they?

Much like with cash equities, this product is probably going to be familiar to most of the readers of this book. An ETF is a fund that is traded on an exchange. This product is available to the general public and is also available to the institutional client of the broker dealer as well. An ETF is a collection of individual cash equities that are grouped together around a common theme. The price of the ETF is derived from the prices of all the individual stocks within it.

Initially when the first ETFs began to make their debut, most were based on an overall stock market index such as the DOW or S&P 500. The ETF would buy up portions of all the stocks contained with the stock market index in the proportion that they appear within the index. For example, if the stock market index contained three stocks with one stock making up 50% of the index and the other two making up 25% each, the same weighting amongst the three stocks would be reflected in the ETF.

ETFs have since evolved beyond their initial roots as being based on the overall stock market indices and now you can find all kinds of specialized ETFs covering a variety of sectors of the overall market. ETFs were initially passive and their composition only varied if the underlying index they were based on varied. However, as the product developed, ETFs that are more actively managed have been introduced and this makes them similar to traditional mutual funds.

In fact, ETFs even at their inception were most commonly compared to mutual funds which like ETFs are a basket of stocks. However, mutual funds are not tradable easily as their value is not calculated throughout the day and only at the end of the day. ETFs however, are priced throughout the day and can be bought and sold just like a stock can at any time the market is open for amounts as little as one share as opposed to mutual funds which may require a minimum investment and have restrictions on when and how they can be redeemed.

ETFs are created from what are called creation units which are formed from a set of securities traded on the exchange. Usually 50,000 shares is the amount in a creation unit but it can vary depending on the ETF. This process starts with an application to the relevant financial authority to create a new ETF. The company sponsoring the creation of the new ETF goes to what is known as an authorized participant like a broker dealer. The broker dealer will acquire the set of securities needed to create the ETF. If for example, it is a fund designed to track a certain index then the broker dealer buys up the shares in the same proportion as they are represented in the index. These shares are given to the ETF issuer. The ETF issuer then gives the broker dealer a block of ETF shares. This block of ETF shares is the creation unit which is equal in value to the shares that the broker dealer gave to the ETF issuer. The broker dealer can then sell these creation units as shares in the ETFs into the market (to both public and institutional investors alike) breaking them up into a little as one share which would represent 1/ 50,000 of the creation unit's total value.

In reality, the EFT shares you buy on the market are legal claims on the ownership of all the shares in the creation unit. The original shares the ETF issuer has remain in trust and are not traded as they form the basis of the ETF. They are not impacted by the trading of the ETF units on the market and indeed the only real things that need to be managed in the creation units are corporate actions like dividends and stock splits. Now all this is pretty detailed but it is useful to know as it is one feature of ETFs that institutional investors can take advantage of as we will soon see.

At the broker dealer the sales traders will receive orders to buy or sell an ETF from their clients just as they would with cash equities as we covered earlier. The process is very much the same even though the ETF represents a large amount of different companies contained within it; it is still a single unit and traded as a stock just like any other stock. Much like with cash equities, commissions are charged on the buying and selling of ETFs.

• • •

5.2. Why do clients buy this product?

Even though the ETF as a product is very suitable for individual retail investors, institutional investors find them just as desirable as a product for a lot of the same reasons.

Representative:

An ETF is representative of a large sector of the stock market or the entire stock market itself. This allows the institutional client of the broker dealer to quickly and easily take up a broad position in a certain sector of the market without having to manage the buy and or sell orders for all the individual stocks within the sector. The ETF does charge management fees of its own and the institutional client will also have to pay commission fees to the broker dealer as well, but the speed and convenience of quickly taking up positions in fast changing sectors throughout the trading day and then being able to exit those positions quickly outweigh the extra cost of the management fee.

Tradable Anytime:

The feature allowing the ETF to be traded at anytime allows the institutional investor the flexibility of buying up a sector as noted above in the morning and then selling the position in that sector a few minutes or hours later. This offers up potentially thousands of trading opportunities for institutional investors that had not existed before ETFs came on the scene.

Six

Equity Research and Research Sales

6.1. What is it?

Equity research is the key content portion of what a broker dealer offers to its clients. There are two main parts to this; equity research and research sales. These two are related to one another but function differently. Let's look at equity research first since it is the starting point. Research analysts work within the research section of the investment bank while not being a front office revenue center in a true sense they still generate a lot of revenue indirectly as we will see. Each analyst is assigned to cover a certain sector of the economy and certain companies or "names" within that sector. Usually the analysts will cover large cap stocks as they are the ones that have the largest trading volumes. In addition, they will also cover the firms that the majority of their clients are interested in. Their job is to develop recommendations and trading ideas for clients for the set of companies that they are assigned to cover using the fundamental, technical and market sentiment factors in their analysis. The ideas and recommendations are included in reports the research analyst is responsible for creating. These reports are distributed to clients as well as distributed to the research sales force that we will discuss in a minute. The research analyst is expected to be an expert in their sector and in the firms that they cover knowing the minute details of the firm, their business and especially their earnings potential which, as we noted, is the key fundamental factor driving stock prices.

In addition to the research analyst, there is also what is known as the macro analyst. This type of analyst covers high level issues and trends in the economy in general. They look at changes in government policy, changes in the economy and news events to try to predict how this will impact the markets as a whole and offer this insight to clients. They do not get involved with the fine details of individual companies and instead their research reports are all focused on the economy and how it, as a whole, will perform. Just as with the analysts who cover specific companies within a sector; the macro analyst is also expected to produce reports for client consumption for the area he covers.

Equity research analysts are expected to deal with clients as well even though their main focus is producing research for clients. Often a client will ask for a meeting with a research analyst to discuss a report giving the analyst the chance to establish creditability with clients and a chance to build trust with the client. However, the analyst cannot spend all day focused on clients, so to help handle this they partner up with the research sales staff whom we will cover now.

Research sales as a function is primarily concerned with two key things, knowing the clients and knowing the firm. The staff in this area will be assigned to cover a set of institutional clients. In terms of dealing with these clients, their entire role revolves around getting to know their clients and building a relationship with them. This relationship building is based on knowing what the client is interested in, their investment style, what types of risks they are able to take, and their needs and desires. In terms of knowing the firm, research sales staff have to know what the firm has to offer clients. Their job is to tailor the research offerings the analysts produce screening what is available, finding what the client is interested in and bringing that to the client's attention. The research sales staff match the client's needs with the services the firm has to offer and market these as solutions to client needs all in order to generate orders for the firm. While the research sales person and the sales trader seem to have similar jobs as both are involved in selling and pitching trade ideas there is a difference. The sales trader is the market specialist and focuses on that aspect providing the client with advice on what is happening in the market and how that might affect their trade in a particular stock. The research sales person is more focused on the individual companies and knows the ins and outs of those companies.

The research itself was not directly "sold" to the clients as a concrete tangible product with a price attached to it but instead it is "bundled" as part of the commission fees charged on trades made. The research sales staff are all geared toward encouraging the client to place orders with the firm for various products and services. The research sales teams present the client with "content" in the form of research and ideas and then the client acts on those with the sales traders (and or execution traders) who "execute" on the ideas. This in turn generates commissions for the broker dealer. So if there are no concrete fees for research how can the broker dealer measure up how well their research sales efforts are going?

Clients rate the broker dealers that they deal with in what are known as "broker reviews". It is like a report card or a health check on what that client thinks of the broker dealer as a whole. The client considers the broker dealer's services in both content and execution and lets the broker dealer know what the client thinks of them in the various categories of services and will rate them according to their competitors. The client will gather up the comments and ratings for all the people in their organization that deal with the broker dealer and put them into a formal official review document to be discussed with the sales people at the broker dealer. For example, a broker dealer might be told that they are number one for the client in single stock cash equities but only rank forth in programs. The broker dealer will not be told which other brokers rank where but the broker dealer can usually figure out who are the number one and number two ranked competitors. These rankings will be compared to the previous year's broker review and the broker dealer can see where they may have improved in the client's eyes or where they may have fallen short. The client will also detail the amount of commission paid for each service and will sometimes let the broker dealer know the total commissions that the client paid to the "street" (all other broker dealers). The broker dealer is thus able to know how much of the client's "wallet" (market share) they have and in what products and services.

The main goal of the broker dealer is to capture a higher ranking in the broker reviews especially for the clients that pay out large commissions to the street. In general, higher rankings should result in higher commissions paid out to the top broker dealers. Some clients have instituted rough guidelines around how much of a percentage of their commissions will be paid out to the top three or top five broker dealers. Perhaps a client may apportion roughly 50% of the total commission to be awarded to the top five firms and the remaining 50% to all the rest. Clients can deal with in excess of 20-25 broker dealers so getting in to that top five means more revenue for the broker dealer.

The results of the broker review are also analyzed from within the broker dealer. After seeing the results and details of the review, they can see how much the client pays out in total and where they rank amongst other broker dealers the client deals with. Internally, service levels will be measured by sales related activities like phone calls and meetings with clients by the sales staff against the commission levels received to produce metrics. This will help the broker dealer better target the best clients to service for maximum revenue.

Before we finish this section we want to touch on one other aspect of commissions and how they work. When clients are offered research ("content") instead of just execution only this is known in the industry as "soft dollars" or "soft commission". In this arrangement the commission fees charged are higher than would be the case for just a simple trade execution. Conversely, "hard dollars" are commission based on execution only and it is measured based on the value of the trades done. However, when the content part represented by research is included in the price of the trade, it is not easy to figure out how much of the commission from a trade is for the "execution" part and how much is the "content" part. When the client receives research they may or may not trade based on that report or the ideas contained within and if they do place an order how much of the trade is due to the research received? There is no way to know and thus the trades may or may not be connected to the research received. It has been argued that this lacks transparency and makes it hard for clients like asset managers or pension funds to explain what the costs (execution versus research) are for running the fund and managing the assets to their clients.

In order to better provide transparency around commissions, the broker dealers and their clients enter in to what is known as a commission sharing agreement (CSA) as it is known in the UK, or a client commission agreement (CCA) as it is known in the US. This is a standing agreement to split the commission on trades into an "execution" part and a "content" part that is supposed to pay for research. If a client has been paying a standard rate of 15 basis points -as in our example in the single stock cash equities section above- when trading the agreement might state that 5 basis points of the 15 be considered execution commission that the executing broker dealer will keep. The other 10 basis points would be commission for "content" that will be kept in a separate account or "pot". As the client trades more with the broker dealer, the amount of money in the "content" account will of course grow. The client is able to "spend" this commission by allocating it to pay for research to which ever firms provided the client with research. They may direct that some of the money be sent to an independent third party research firm that has provided them with research but has not executed any trades for them. The broker dealer will then have to send this money to the third party research firm. Likewise, a broker dealer that did not execute any trades for the client might receive a payment for research from another broker dealer who did execute trades. Alternatively, the client may direct some of the commission in this account to the broker dealer that executes the trades to pay for research from that same broker dealer. Clients will setup several CCA / CSAs with various broker dealers meaning that there are a lot of possible payment scenarios being made back and forth between all the parties to the agreements depending on how the client allocates the commissions. This does create more administrative work for all parties concerned but the idea is that this CCA and CSA model provides clarity around what part of the commission is being used for what and who is being paid for research. In the future this model will probably develop further and we might one day see a complete split between execution and content and how they are paid for by clients.

• • •

6.2. Why are clients interested in this?

As mentioned, the client is not really "buying" a concrete and separate product as it is part of the price of the trade commission. The broker dealer and the analysts within it are competing with all the other investment banks and their analysts. The research or "content" product has to be top notch and desirable to clients. Clients are bombarded with research offerings from all the broker dealers they deal with and independent research providers as well. From a client's point of view this is a lot of "noise" to try to work through to find one or two good ideas that they can use. The client is looking for an edge that will help them perform better. At the end of the day, it is important to remember that all the institutional clients manage money on behalf of someone else and those end clients want to see their investments and assets grow in value and investment managers are accountable for that. Anything that can help a client reach that goal is what they are looking for in the "content" offered by the broker dealer. Innovative new ideas and different ways of looking at the markets and the stocks within are highly valued by the clients because news travels fast and soon enough ideas that worked well in the recent past are rendered useless as other market participants find out about it and jump in. Likewise, accurate predictions and insight on the future prices of stocks and a track record of delivering on that are highly valued by clients.

For the research analysts and research sales staff this means knowing your client's needs and consistently delivering on those needs. Clients will read the research reports from the analysts and answer calls from the research sales people with whom they have built a successful relationship with. Reports that get read by clients get the analyst's work in front of the clients; calls taken get the trading ideas in front of the client. All this leads to more orders for the broker dealer with more commissions and more revenue.

Seven

Program Trading

7.1. What is it?

As opposed to cash equities which we covered earlier, programs trading involves trading a basket of securities instead of just one. This is defined by the New York Stock Exchange as 15 or more securities with a value of over $1 million dollars. The basket of stocks to be traded is sometimes also known as a "basket order", or a "basket trade", these terms mean the same as program trading. You may also hear the term portfolio trading as well.

Regardless of the name, this type of product started being offered in the 1970s when computer technology was able to handle these large volume and complex orders. Indeed computers are a key part of a programs trade as they are used to execute the trade. A program trade is a large volume trade and all the components within the basket are intended to be traded simultaneously and as such it needs to be handled differently from the cash equities business even though the program trade is composed of a set of single stock cash equities. Computer programs trade the actual contents of the program trade much like the execution trader does for a single stock cash equity. Since there are a lot of stocks involved in the program order there is no way an execution trader can manage all the orders; cutting them up and submitting them to the market for execution at times when the prices look favorable. Given this, the program as a whole is submitted to be traded by computer via algorithms designed to trade little parts of the overall program throughout the day when prices or market conditions meet certain criteria. The use of computer programs in this process is where the term "program trading" originated.

Sales traders specialized in handling these types of orders are usually arranged into a "programs" trading team much like how the single stock cash equities traders are arranged into a team. The client will send in an order with all the details of the stocks to be traded. Just like with single stock trades, clients will assign trading instructions such as price limits to the stocks within the basket. The client will negotiate with the program sales trader on the overall commission rates to be charged to the client. Since each program is very large compared to a single stock order and is different in terms of size and content there is far more room for negotiation over commission rates as opposed to single stock orders which are generally treated roughly the same in terms of commission (although there can be some price negotiation). The sales trader handling these orders will offer up a commission rate quoted in basis points and the client will consider it against what other broker dealers have offered as well.

What makes it different from a single stock order is that a large volume of stocks and their trades are being handled at the same time and the order management system is designed to be able to report the program as a whole and the performance of those trades as a whole. Some parts of the portfolio will perform really well and others may not but the client is usually looking for the overall performance on the program as a whole and will judge the broker dealer on that. Much like with a single stock order, the quality of the execution is measured by getting the best prices.

Finally, it is important to note that while a program is made up of single stocks it can also contain ETFs which as we saw can be traded just as easily as a single stock can. Also, a program can contain equity futures and equity options within it in addition to single stocks. There are a wide variety of combinations available to clients depending on their needs.

In the previous section we looked at ETFs and how they work and what they are. We want to return to that topic as it ties in with programs trading. Some of the clients of the broker dealer are asset managers that in turn offer ETF products to their end clients. When these companies are changing the holdings within their ETF portfolios this can result in a large amount of orders, these orders can come into the broker dealer in the form of programs orders.

• • •

7.2. Why do clients buy this product?

Risk Management:

Trading in stocks is risky as they can be volatile as the future prices are always uncertain. Program trading is used to manage some of the risks associated with trading. The idea of a program trade is that all the stocks within the program are traded at the same time. Fund managers need to manage both the shares that they hold and also the proportion of the shares that they hold across many sectors of the economy in relation to each other within their portfolios. In order to do this they often need to conduct a lot of trades in a day to maintain this balance. Trading these shares one at time makes it hard to manage the risk of price movements in the shares that are not being traded yet. A programs trade allows for the simultaneous trading of all the stocks in the same time period ensuring that any sudden price movements that the fund manager or the sales trader might feel are due to happen in the very near future are avoided.

In addition to this, a program of trades can be used to help hedge a position. A client might set up a series of buy orders in one program and have a series of short sell orders in another program to counter balance the risk of his buy orders. The stocks involved in each program are not necessarily the same and may be quite different. In some cases a buy offer for say one computer manufacturer may be hedged with a short sell in another computer manufacturer, this can also happen between various sectors of the economy as well, buy one and short sell the other. The programs trade allows the clients access to an unlimited combination of ways to hedge their positions in the market.

This allows the client to respond to market conditions and opportunities as well to help quickly manage exposure to various segments of the market. The set of stocks to be included in a program trade is determined by the client based on their goals and they are able to match up what they want to buy and sell adding them to a basket and then trade them. This helps them manage risk as opposed to buying a single stock one order at a time.

Reduced costs:

Trading in larger volumes usually results in much cheaper costs to the institutional investor and this is especially the case with a programs trade order. Broker dealers are keen to get these large volume orders as it can represent a large amount of commission for them even if the commission rates are much lower than those for individual single stock cash equities. Broker dealers also benefit from the increased trading volume which is one of the ways in which they are judged. Being amongst the top firms in terms of trading volume on an exchange is a valued achievement that the broker dealer aims for as it conveys the power and influence of the broker dealer and this in turn leads to more clients coming to do business with the broker dealer.

Speedier trading and ease of changing positions quickly:

Creating a basket of stocks and trading them as a program allows for speedier trading and allows institutional clients to quickly change positions. This allows the client to respond to market conditions and opportunities as well to help quickly manage exposure to various segments of the market. An example of this is when a client would like to exit a portfolio quickly and transition from one portfolio to another. This is known as transition management. The client will put together the portfolio to be sold and the portfolio to be bought and submit them to the broker dealer as a program trade. This transition from one portfolio to another can happen all at once all at the same time.

Eight

Direct Market Access / Algorithm Trading

8.1. What is it?

Direct Market Access (also known as "DMA" or "Electronic Trading") is an execution product offering in which the broker dealer gives clients access to the exchange and the order book on the exchange (the complete set of the buy and sell orders). Normally clients come to the broker dealer as they are licensed to trade on the exchange and have access to the order book. However, DMA allows the client access to the exchange via the infrastructure of the broker dealer. The clients simply "rent" the broker dealer's infrastructure to access the exchange and are responsible for their own trades. This is also known as an "execution only" type of product as there is no content offered to the client. The client does not deal with a sales trader who can provide them with colour on the market. There is no contact with research salespeople who would offer up expertise and advice on the markets and trading ideas. There is also no execution trader that offers trading expertise as well. The concept of content is missing from the DMA product offering which is why it is sometimes referred to as a "low touch" service (as the broker dealer's staff do not "touch" the order) as opposed to the "high touch" service of a sales trader. Since there is no content offered there is no "bundled" fee for research as found with a single stock cash equity trade placed through a sales trader. Thus DMA is priced cheaper when offered to clients. However, just as with the single stock cash equity, the fee is charged in basis points on any trading transactions the client makes.

Much like with the technological developments that allowed program trading to arise, the same applies to DMA as a product. The development of networks and powerful computing allowed more ways to trade electronically and trade quickly. DMA grew out of this as did algorithm trading. Algorithm trading is a product usually tied in closely with DMA as a product offering which is why we have included them together. Broker dealers have developed a lot of algorithms to assist with trading. The algorithm basically does what the execution trader does; it slices up the orders into pieces and enters them into the market at times when market conditions seem good. The algorithms will determine the prices and quantities to trade on based on a variety of quantitative data the algorithm looks at. Recent trades made on the market by others, past trading volumes, current prices and other data sources are used as inputs into the algorithm. These inputs are then used in complex mathematical formulas which determine what amounts to trade and when to trade them. The algorithms can react to information faster than human traders can and can manage far more orders than a human trader can which is why algorithms are a major part of the way programs trades are executed as noted when we looked at programs trades.

Clients are able to select from a selection of algorithms that offer up different strategies. The broker dealer will market these strategies as part of its DMA product offering. The broker dealer of course does not reveal the contents of the algorithm nor how it works but markets the results of the algorithm to clients. The contents of the algorithms are highly protected by broker dealers to protect their competitive advantage over the offerings of other broker dealers.

The use of DMA and algorithms has resulted in an explosion of trading in the past few years. Algorithms are able to respond far faster than any human will ever be able to and the more complex algorithms are able to take in news from news articles or social media and weigh the news or comments as either positive or negative and include that as an input into the mathematical calculations that determine how the order will be sliced up and sent to the market for execution.

So how would a client use this DMA product to place orders for execution? Well the first thing is that the broker dealer will discuss the DMA service offerings with the client and all the terms and conditions will be laid out. Once the client agrees the broker dealer will next take the client through the onboarding process. What this means is that the client will be onboarded on to the broker dealer's infrastructure and provided with access. Broker dealers and their clients communicate with each other through an industry standard messaging system known as FIX. FIX is a communications protocol that lays out all the standardized data that needs to be communicated when orders are placed from clients to broker dealers such as prices and quantities. The broker dealer usually has an onboarding team of specialists that take care of all this. Once the client is onboarded they are ready to trade. The client will be responsible for all their orders and traders within the clients will trade these orders and route them into the algorithms or even execute them manually should they choose like an execution trader at the broker dealer would. The broker dealer will provide support for the client's trades and be there to troubleshoot should any issues arise between the broker dealer, the client and the exchange. Instead of facing off to research sales and sales trading staff, the DMA using client generally faces off to more technical and IT focused staff within the broker dealer.

• • •

8.2. Why do clients buy this product?

Cost:

DMA does not contain any content and there is little interaction with the broker dealer for content. The broker dealer is thus able to offer greatly reduced commission rates to clients but in exchange for lower commission fees the client is responsible for all their own trading.

Client Control:

Since the client handles the orders themselves and submits them to the exchange directly they are in full control of the order and its execution. They can cancel it if they like, change the price conditions and any other aspect of the order. The traders at the client are able to react at any time to changing market conditions much faster than going through a sales trader which would slow things down.

Automation and Decision Making Speed:

Algorithms make it so that changes in information can be reacted to almost instantaneously. Human intervention in the trade is not needed. Information on prices and quantities available for buy and sell orders on the exchanges changes 1000s of times a second and there is no way that humans can react that fast to the changes. Thus, decision making is given to the algorithms that take over and trade based on the information that comes in from the markets. In addition to this, many broker dealers offer low latency or ultra low latency direct market access which reduces the delay in information coming in to the algorithm and thus increases the speed at which the algorithms can react to the market. This allows for even more trading opportunities when paired with trading algorithms which can trade 1000s of times a second in what is known as high frequency trading. Ideally these will give the clients more chance to profit (or more potential to lose as well) on the trades that they make.

Nine

Securities Lending

9.1. What is it?

Securities lending is a service offered by the broker dealer to its clients. Usually it is offered as a part of a total set of services known as "Prime Brokerage" or "Prime Services". We will cover that product grouping later on but we want to cover securities lending separately as it is an important concept in and of its own right. In the section on single stock cash equities above we spoke about the concept of selling a stock short; well securities leading is intimately tied to that concept and without it there would be no easy way to sell stocks short. While short selling is now the major use case behind securities lending, originally it arose out of the need to cover settlement failure. An example of this is as follows; we buy some stock from one party and then five minutes later, once the price has moved to a point where we can make a profit, we sell it to another party. In order for this transaction to succeed the person we bought it from needs to deliver the stock to us so that we can deliver it to the person we sold it to. However, the person we bought the stock from fails to deliver it to us so we cannot deliver it to the person we sold it to. Both of us are in breach but in order to rectify our breach of the trade we can borrow securities from someone else to cover our part of the trade until the securities owed to us arrive. Once the securities owed to us arrive, we will repay them to the person we borrowed them from. Even though short selling has far surpassed settlement failure as a reason to borrow securities, settlement failures still occur and borrowing is still used to resolve these situations.

Like with any loan there are two sides to the transaction; the lender and the borrower. First let's take a look at the lender who acts as the source of supply for the securities loans. The lender is usually a large institution with a lot of different security holdings and one that tends to hold these securities over long periods of time. Pension funds and insurance companies are prime examples of the type of institution that would be willing to loan out their securities. The large institutions that lend out the securities will usually employ an agent to handle all aspects of security lending. Agents might be the custodian for the investment manager or perhaps a third party firm that specializes in securities lending.

Borrowing firms on the other hand vary considerably from hedge funds, banks, other insurance companies, and of course the broker dealer itself. The broker dealer may borrow the securities for their own purposes, or they will offer them to their clients as part of the prime brokerage suite of services.

Regardless of who borrows the securities and for what purpose, a master securities lending agreement needs to be established between the borrowers and the lenders. This contract will cover all the terms of the agreement including the main details around which securities are to be loaned out and what the collateral requirements of the borrowers are and of course the fees.

So let's look at an example of this in action. A large pension fund with a lot of holdings has tasked their custodian to lend out the securities they hold to willing borrowers. The custodian and the pension fund contact a broker dealer and discuss the matter. The broker dealer is interested and the two parties, leader and borrower start to negotiate a securities lending agreement. As part of this agreement, the broker dealer agrees to post up collateral to the lender which is a standard market practice. This collateral is usually in the form of other securities like stocks and bonds or simply cash. Regardless of what the collateral is, it must be worth more than the value of the stocks borrowed. In US markets this is set by regulation at 102% for collateral consisting of domestic stocks and bonds or 105% for foreign stocks and bonds. This collateral will be checked on a daily basis to ensure that it exceeds the value of the securities borrowed by at least 2% (or 5% for foreign stocks) and thus might need adjustment over time depending on the market prices of the securities. The custodian will receive the collateral against the securities loaned out to the broker dealer. In this case the broker dealer uses cash as collateral but they could have used stocks, bonds or any combination of the two. The custodian receives this and is able to invest the cash collateral. The broker dealer and the custodian negotiate how much of the income on the cash collateral is to be rebated to the broker dealer with custodian keeping some of it. The terms of this are included in the master securities lending agreement. Finally the fees; expressed as ever in basis points, are agreed to between the two parties. The fee will vary depending on what the collateral is, basically with cash collateral the fee is the spread on the interest they will earn on the collateral versus what they have to rebate to the borrower. The fee could also be a straight up fee payable in cash and quoted in basis points.

When securities are borrowed, the title or ownership of the securities legally passes to the borrower. This means that the borrower will receive all dividends and voting rights on the securities borrowed. The securities lending agreement will cover this and ensure that the borrower pay back any dividends received on the shares for the duration of the loan. In terms of voting rights, these are lost to the lender and for the duration of the loan the borrower is entitled to them. However, in some cases the lender can add in a clause to the securities lending agreement giving the right for the lender to recall the shares lent out so that the lender can exercise voting rights if they so wish. The circumstances around this and what type of vote it would apply to are stipulated in the lending agreement.

Once the agreement is finalized between the broker dealer as borrower, the custodian as agent and the pension fund as lender; the securities to be lent are delivered to the broker dealer and the broker dealer will deliver the collateral to the custodian who holds it for the pension fund. The custodian will be the one who manages the process between the broker dealer and the end client; the pension fund. In this capacity the custodian provides reporting to both the lender and the borrower throughout the duration of the loan making sure that all operational aspects of the security loan (daily collateral checks, rebates of interest to the broker dealer and receiving any dividend income from the broker dealer) are taken care of.

With the master securities lending agreement in place the broker dealer can now use the borrowed securities as they wish. They may use them for their own purposes or they may turn around and offer security loans to their own clients and as noted this is usually offered as a part of the prime brokerage service. This might typically come about starting with a sales person; perhaps someone in research sales or a sales trader talking to a client about short sale or arbitrage opportunities. If the client is interested the sales staff will refer them to the prime brokerage unit who will start the process to get them set up to borrow securities. Also, the prime brokerage unit has its own sales staff as well that seek to sell securities lending agreements to their clients.

Regardless of who sells it, in order to get the client setup to borrow shares a securities lending agreement with the same type of conditions for collateral, rebates of interest and dividend payments and other terms and conditions is needed. This process is the same as it is for the initial agreement between the broker dealer and the pension fund. It is important to note that the title to the security is with whoever has borrowed them at the end of the chain. So in this case the title passes from the pension fund to the broker dealer who borrows them initially and then finally to the client of the broker dealer who is at the end of the chain of borrowers. This means that the broker dealer has to manage the aspects of the rebate of the interest on the collateral and the receipt of dividend payments between itself and its client as well as between itself and the custodian acting as agent for the original lender; the pension fund. The broker dealer will of course attempt to make a spread in terms of the interest payments on the collateral keeping a larger portion of the interest rebate it receives from the pension fund compared to the amount it has to rebate to its clients on their collateral. In addition to non cash collateral, the broker dealer will charge a fee payable in cash and quoted in basis points just like that the broker dealer has to pay to the pension fund.

Securities lending is a complex process and there are a lot of contractual details that need to be worked out before the process can even begin. Once the process has been agreed on there are a lot of operational issues that need to be conducted throughout the life of the transaction such as the daily check on collateral requirements. In order to make the process smoother, the International Securities Lending Association has made great efforts to better standardize agreements such as that seen in the Global Master Securities Lending Agreement; a boilerplate agreement designed to help make it easy to arrange securities lending agreements.

Single stock cash equities as a product are nowhere near as complex but yet without securities lending there would be no easy way to sell shares short which makes securities lending a vital part of the overall trading of single stock cash equities and why we have devoted a section to it.

• • •

9.2. Why do clients buy this product?

From the borrower's point of view:

As noted, the main reason for a client of the broker dealer to enter into a securities lending agreement is to allow them to short sell.

This opens up all kinds of investment strategies to clients allowing them to arbitrage; a popular example of this involves convertible bonds and buying the convertible and selling the underlying stock short hoping to make a profit on the difference. We also saw the example in which securities lending was used to cover settlement failure. Finally, in some cases, since the voting rights are transferred to the borrower (unless otherwise stated in the contract) the borrower of the securities could use this as a way to gain influence in a company temporarily depending on the situation.

From the lender's point of view:

From the view of a large fund with a lot of stock holdings, lending out securities helps provide extra returns for the portfolio in terms of the fees received from the borrower. The lender keeps the economic rights to the dividend (as the borrower receives it but has to pay it back to the lender) and yet earns a fee for lending out the securities. Also, they can invest the cash collateral and aim to make a profit on the difference they receive versus the amount that they have to rebate to the borrower. From this point of view there is nothing to lose by renting out an asset you have sitting around. However, this is not without risk. There is a risk that the borrower may not return the securities borrowed, or that the borrower may not be able to provide additional collateral when needed. Finally, the return on the cash collateral could not work out in the lender's favor and they could end up paying more out to the borrower than they could earn.

Ten

Prime Brokerage Services

10.1. What is it?

Prime brokerage, also known as prime services, is a set of services offered to clients of the broker dealer. It is mainly targeted at hedge funds and other smaller money managers. Smaller institutional clients do not have the operational infrastructure compared to larger ones like pension funds and insurance companies so the prime brokerage service helps fill that gap helping the hedge fund out by centralizing all their activities and providing support for their trading and capital needs. Prime brokerage services arose in the late 1970s. In those days, hedge funds started to make ever increasing volumes of trades and managing all those became difficult. Broker dealers saw an opportunity to develop a service since they already had experience in managing large volumes of trades as a part of their daily operations anyway. However, support for trading activities is not the only thing that the prime brokerage service offers. So what does the prime brokerage unit offer clients? As we already noted, securities lending is a large part of this; a topic we have already covered but there is far more that the prime brokerage unit offers to hedge fund clients.

Trade support was the initial catalyst for this service. Hedge funds often make many trades throughout the trading day with many different brokers. The problem they have is keeping track of all these trades and making sure that there are no issues. Since hedge funds are smaller institutions they cannot invest in the type of trade support services that larger institutions have thus they can outsource this to the prime brokerage service of a broker dealer. The prime brokerage service provides a consolidated platform for the hedge fund gathering up all their trades and providing trade reporting and support for their trading activities. Trade reporting allows the hedge fund to understand what its positions are and the value of those positions even if held at different broker dealers. Support is also offered to help with trade settlement and the prime broker can handle dealing with the other broker dealers that the hedge fund trades with in terms of settlement and trade confirmation and trade processing activities. The prime brokerage unit takes fees on these trade support services based on commissions from the trades done by the hedge fund client at the broker dealer and they also collect fees for providing settlement services for other trades done with other broker dealers.

Custody services may also be offered to the hedge fund. What this means is that the prime broker will act as a custodian for the holdings of the hedge fund holding the assets on behalf of the hedge fund, ensuring that settlement and delivery of shares takes place. The custody service will also take care of any corporate actions on stocks the hedge fund holds such as stock splits or stock dividends. Tax issues arising from income on dividends and or cash assets are also services that fall within the type of services a prime brokerage offers. Basically, the custody service consists of a lot of the day to day administration issues that arise from the assets held by the hedge fund everything from accounting, to tax, to legal and compliance issues are dealt with. The fees charged for this service would be based on the assets in custody usually in the form of a basis point fee on the value of the assets held in custody.

Another major service offered by the prime brokerage unit is financing. The securities lending aspect we covered earlier is usually considered as part of the "financing" suite of services. However, the prime broker can also help the hedge fund arrange financing either by leading them money directly or arranging for more traditional financing like a bank loan. The prime broker can tie this in with the custody services offered using those assets held in custody as collateral on the financing arrangements made on behalf of the hedge fund. This helps provide the hedge fund with borrowed capital which in turn the hedge fund can use as leverage to increase their trading returns. The prime brokerage unit faces risks when offering financing to hedge funds. For example, if they have helped to finance a hedge fund and the hedge fund suffers large trading losses, it might not be able to return the borrowed funds to the prime broker or not be able to maintain the collateral requirements. The risk of funding the trading activity of hedge fund clients needs to be balanced off against the benefit that financing them allows them to trade more which brings in more commission fees to the broker dealer as a whole. The broker dealer will also earn money on the financing spread offered to the clients by perhaps sourcing the funds from an external source and then charging the client a higher rate. Also, we saw that the prime broker can offer securities lending to hedge fund clients and hopefully earn a profit on the spread between what they can get on the cash collateral and what they have to rebate to the borrowing hedge funds.

To help the hedge fund manage this risk and continue to stay in business, the prime broker also offers a risk management service. The prime brokerage unit monitors the holdings of the hedge fund client and puts these through a series of risk scenarios designed to determine what the value of the client's holdings would be if certain events were to happen in the market. These risk scenarios also calculate how long it would take to completely liquidate a holding without having to quickly sell it off which would put downwards pressure on the price. These are then used to "stress test" the portfolio to find its breaking points, the points at which the risk becomes too great. These points are in turn used by the prime broker to establish what it feels are safe limits on the amount of financing it can provide to a hedge fund.

Finally, there is one area that the prime broker provides as a service and this is known as capital introduction. Hedge funds need to seek out investors to provide them with the capital that they will use to trade and hopefully, if successful, provide a return on that capital to the investor and collect a fee for doing so. The prime brokerage unit offers a service that attempts to help hedge funds find that capital. This is what capital introduction is all about. So how does it work?

Well to start with, the hedge fund must be at least performing and have a track record of providing returns to clients otherwise without this there is no point for the prime broker to introduce a hedge fund with a poor track record as no one is going to want to invest in it. What the capital introduction team seeks to do is find suitable investors for their hedge fund clients. They specialize in this area and have a lot of knowledge and experience with what the current trends are and know what potential investors are looking for. Just like with fashion trends, there are also trends in investing and certain investment strategies fall in and out of favor depending on what happens in the markets.

Likewise, the capital introduction team is expected to know what their hedge fund clients do and their investment style so that they can help the hedge fund position itself in the market. Competitor analysis is a part of this and the capital introduction team will discuss this with the hedge fund client allowing them to understand what other hedge funds are doing or trying to do in the market. Once the initial analysis is done, the capital introduction staff will plan out a target list of prospective investors seeking to match up the investor type and style with that of the hedge fund. After this is done they will assist the hedge fund by arranging meetings with investors on a one to one basis. Also, the capital introduction team will usually have a few large scale events that they run regularly throughout the year that they use to bring investors and hedge funds together. Once the meetings are arranged, the capital introduction team will assist the hedge fund in preparing the marketing materials and presentations for the investors. Should this process be successful, the hedge fund will find itself with new investors and new capital to manage. The prime broker and the capital introduction team will not usually charge any fees for the capital introduction service but the expected result is that the hedge fund will trade more with the broker dealer as a whole and thus the result is increased commissions for the broker dealer.

・・・

10.2. Why do clients buy this product?

Hedge funds come to the prime broker for the support that the prime broker is able to offer. For newly starting off hedge funds, the prime broker is able to provide the hedge fund with the infrastructure needed to start out in terms of trade support. Some prime brokerage units will even help clients find office space as well, aiding their clients with their physical infrastructure needs.

As the hedge fund starts up and begins trading more and more, the prime brokerage provides the infrastructure needed to short sell, helps the fund manage risk and helps provide financing to allow the fund to magnify its returns and develop a successful track record. That successful track record can then lead to capital introductions with potential investors. It could be argued that the modern hedge fund industry owes its existence to the services provided by the prime brokerage business units at the broker dealer. While hedge funds did exist before the prime brokerage business started up, the boom in hedge funds only started after the broker dealers began offering more support to their clients and facilitating their businesses.

Eleven

Crossing

11.1. What is it?

Crossing is an execution service offered to the clients of a broker dealer. A cross is a trade conducted between two parties, one party wants to sell and one party wants to buy. The two parties will agree to a price and conduct the transaction without doing it on the stock exchange. This is the key difference; a cross trade is off exchange trade as opposed to a trade which is done on an exchange. With a cross trade the desired price is set first usually using some price based on the prices in the exchange such as the daily volume weighted average price, or perhaps a midpoint price between the bid and ask prices and then the trade is executed using this price. Crossing in this way gives the clients the option to access an alternative execution venue other than that found on the exchange and can allow for better prices. Of course if there is no one to cross with at the desired price then no trade execution occurs.

Initially crossing started within the broker dealer itself as two sales traders would cross their clients' buy and sell orders internally. Broker dealers started to create in house internal crossing systems to provide a venue for their clients to cross trades in. As broker dealers consolidated and grew larger, the volume of trade flow that they handled increased and in turn they could offer more opportunities to cross.

Eventually, other firms started to setup crossing networks outside of the broker dealer's in house networks and opened them up making crossing available to more market participants. Now there are various venues for crossing trades, some owned by independent companies, some by broker dealers and even some are offered by the exchanges. You may have heard of the term "dark pool". Basically a dark pool is trading venue were trades can take place but the prices are not visible to anyone, the price quotations that market participants are willing to trade at are invisible and so are the quantities available to trade. This is where the concept of them being "dark" comes from. There are no buy and sell orders visible. So if the prices are invisible how can anyone cross trades inside them? Let's look at an example of how this works.

When an order is received by the sales traders they will check to see if the client is willing to cross their orders and at what price they are willing to cross at. In most cases the clients are willing to consider crossing orders off exchange if they can get a better price and this is a very common practice. The sales traders will split up the client's order into little pieces and send these out through the network to these crossing venues / dark pools sending what is known as an indicator of interest to them. This is not an order to buy or sell but it is like an alert showing that some party is interested in trading. The IOI will contain the price, the stock name, if it is a buy or a sell order and the quantity but it is completely anonymous and it is not a commitment to trade whereas placing this on an exchange is a commitment to trade. Responses to the IOI from within the pool can then lead to the actual order being sent in and the crossing systems will then cross the trades at the prices the buying and selling clients desire. The cross might consist of a lot of small transactions with lots of counterparties as the order has been cut up into many small pieces. Once the crossing is completed, the clients are informed of the details including the prices and quantities for each execution. Of course the broker dealer will charge a fee for this service in exactly the same way they would for a single stock cash equity trade with the fee, as always, quoted in basis points.

Single stocks can be crossed against one another but crossing with programs orders is also possible as the individual orders for the stocks within the program as treated the same as a single stock and are cut up and send out to the crossing venues seeking another trade to cross with. The only difference is that a crossing a full programs order involves a lot more transactions because of the number of securities involved. Any crosses made are then communicated to the clients. With programs crossing the basis point commission structure is still used on the trades that the clients end up crossing. Programs orders tend to be crossed more than single stock orders simply because they are so large that they have more opportunity to cross and there is also more incentive to cross them as large orders in the market can affect prices whereas sending them to be crossed can avoid this. Likewise, large single stock trades of over 10,000 shares known as "block trades" are also prime candidates for crossing for the same reasons.

Crossing usually takes place early in the morning before the markets open for the morning session. Since there is no market activity at that point in time the clients might look to see what is available to cross by sending out IOIs into the crossing venues and looking at what comes back and they might decide to cross if they find something that looks good. After the market has opened, crossing can of course take place at any time during the trading day and while it is more common in the morning, it is not restricted to just the morning.

It is important to note that there are various restrictions around crossing depending on the jurisdiction. Certain jurisdictions allow crossing and others do not. Even if crossing is allowed there might be certain restrictions on the price limits that can be agreed to between two parties attempting to cross. Also, the cross will have to be reported to the regulators in a timely manner even though it did not actually take place on an exchange. All these varied restrictions attempt to ensure that the securities markets remain fair and transparent.

11.2. Why do clients buy this product?

Liquidity:

Crossing offers an alternative source of liquidity, liquidity meaning that an asset can be sold quickly and cash received without having its price affected too much. Remember that supply and demand affect the price of equities in the market place just like they do for anything else in life. In the public markets the liquidity is visible and published thus some market participants can take up positions to affect prices. This of course affects the price that the buyer or seller will get for their asset. If a client submits a large sell order into the market, it is going to adversely cause the price to drop as the supply of the stock has increased. This means that the client will receive less for those shares. However, going to a crossing venue or dark pool can offer better liquidity in that the stock can be sold quickly without having an impact on price as much as in a public market.

Cost:

Crossing can help the clients reduce trading transaction costs. If a cross can be done at the midpoint between the buy price and sell price, the spread is reduced thus reducing the cost for the trade. Likewise, exchange fees can be avoided in a cross since it does not take place on an exchange. Clients are also better able to negotiate lower commission fees with broker dealers on crossed trades.

Information Leakage:

Crossing is anonymous and thus it is harder for market participants to find out what is going on in the market since everything is not visible. Information is power and if market participants know that there is a large sell order out there on the exchange then they know the price is most likely going to go down because of the increased supply just as we noted above. The advance knowledge of knowing a large order is out there can further magnify the market price impact affect ahead of the sale even happening. Other market participants might sell their holdings of the stock or short sell the stock to take advantage of the expected drop in price that this large order will cause. Conversely, for a large buy order that is known to be out there the market participants can buy the stock ahead of time to take advantage of this, bidding up the price before this large order even trades. So not only does the large order itself trigger a price impact due to the change in supply and demand, but it also triggers speculative trades trying to take advantage of this. Crossing helps remove this risk by keeping the information hidden.

Twelve

Facilitation and Market Making

12.1. What is it?

Market making and facilitation are two similarity related concepts. Basically, it is all about providing liquidity to the market for the equities involved thus allowing for trades to be executed on said equities. It offers clients another way to execute their order.

Market making is when a broker dealer helps "make the market" for an equity. The broker dealer will hold shares of the equity for sale and likewise will buy the equity from sellers who wish to sell it. The broker dealer provides price quotes for the bid and ask prices and competes with other broker dealers for trade flow in the form of orders. The broker dealer is expected to honor the price that is quoted. In order to do this, the broker dealer has to maintain a large inventory of shares available for trade. Therefore, it is important that the cost of shares in inventory is, on average, below the current share price being offered otherwise the broker dealer is going to lose money. In addition, being a market maker means tying up your own capital in an inventory of shares thus losing the opportunity to use that capital for something else. Because the broker dealer is using their own money while market making this is known as "dealing" as there is no brokering transaction by acting purely as an agent for clients as would in the case of going to the exchange. This type of transaction is also called a "principal" transaction as the client is dealing directly with the broker dealer in a trade involving the broker dealer's own capital.

So why would the broker dealer engage in this, what is in it for them? The broker dealer makes money when it acts as a market maker on the spread between the buy and sell prices. The broker dealer will, for example, post up a buy price of say $10.00 a share and a sell price of $10.05 a share. That five cents a share is the spread that the market maker will earn. The broker dealer will base the prices offered on how much they bought the stock for in the first place and of course how much other broker dealers are pricing that stock for.

When acting as a market maker, the broker dealer can sell these shares to clients or to other broker dealers as well. The broker dealer can potentially earn a lot on that spread relative to the cost of the shares in inventory if they are able to buy from and sell to clients rapidly. The higher the turnover in transactions in the stock, the more the broker dealer can make.

Client facilitation is similar to market making, the client will buy or sell with the broker dealer instead of going to the exchange to find a counterparty to trade with. The broker acts as a dealer in this case just as with market making. However, client facilitation is more customized; for example, a client might approach the broker directly seeking a source of liquidity to execute on a trade that is not offered as part of the market making the broker dealer is doing. Facilitation is most often encountered with block trades. A block trade is when a client wants to buy or sell a large number of shares which if put on the market, would cause a large price movement. If the client has not been able to find a way to offload the block trade either on the exchange, or through a crossing network, the client might attempt to have the broker dealer facilitate the order for them.

The client negotiates the price with the broker dealer (just like with a program trade they will probably shop around for the best price amongst broker dealers) and if the broker dealer agrees to the terms and is able to facilitate the trade, the broker dealer becomes the counterparty to the trade. As with market making, the broker dealer is going to try to make a profit on the difference between what they buy the shares from the client for and the price they will get reselling the shares in the market. The broker dealer will employ numerous ways to analyze what the best price to give to the client would be and still hopefully make a profit later on.

In addition to the block trade example above, there could be more complex and customized trades involving other products like derivatives or swaps that the client might come to the broker to help execute on.

Finally, it is important to note that broker dealers can offer market making and client facilitation on listed stocks that are traded on the stock exchanges or on over the counter stocks. Over the counter stocks are those too small or those that do not meet exchange requirements to be listed. This is where the market making and facilitation really comes into play as there is no exchange to go to in order to trade them, one of the only ways might be to go to the broker dealer.

• • •

12.2. Why do clients buy this product?

Alternative Source of Liquidity:

Much like with crossing, market making and facilitation offers clients an alternative venue to seek liquidity in and to achieve the price that they wish to trade at without having to trade on the exchange and perhaps receive an adverse price especially for block trades involving tens of thousands of shares. Doing so on the market would cause the price to collapse if they wanted to sell, or if they wanted to buy, would cause the price to skyrocket. Also, the client might be trading in a stock that is illiquid on the main market and there are not many market participants trading it. If the client deals with the broker dealer directly as a counter party, they can find a potential source of liquidity through the broker dealer that is not available on the public stock exchanges.

Risk Management:

When the broker dealer is used as the counterparty, the client can transfer the price risk to the broker dealer instead of having to take risk on the exchange. It could take time for a client to complete a trade on the exchange at the price they wish. Any news developments in that time can cause large movements in the prices that affect the price the client can get. Getting a broker dealer to facilitate that trade can get the client a more stable price and get the trade executed in a timelier manner. This is especially desirable if the client needs to raise cash quickly; perhaps the client is undergoing a lot of withdrawals from their funds by their end clients and need to sell securities quickly and ensure that they are executed quickly. The risk of waiting for a sell order to go through the market and be completed might be too great a risk to take.

Broker dealers have systems in place that can help the traders calculate the risk to themselves should they take on the order from the client. These systems help the broker dealer calculate how many days it might take to unload the trade and at what price they would be willing to accept being counterparty for a client at. The overall experience of the broker dealer in the markets allows them to make these judgments.

Better Prices:

Market participants can obtain better prices with the broker dealer as counterparty to their trades either as market makers or during client facilitation. As noted, they can avoid some of the pricing risks but also the network of market making broker dealers ensures that there is competition in the pricing of equities. Broker dealers competing amongst each other and with the exchanges; provide more pricing opportunities for market participants than without them.

Thirteen

Corporate Access

13.1. What is it?

Corporate access is a content related service provided to clients of the broker dealer. It is not involved with execution nor providing liquidity. Corporate access brings together clients of the broker dealer with the management teams of the companies listed on the exchanges. The broker dealer provides "management access" for the clients. In corporate access terms, clients of the broker dealer are known as "investors" because they, as we noted at the start, take the capital that they are entrusted to manage and invest it. The companies that the investors invest in are known as "corporates". In the corporate access world it is all about bringing the investors together with the corporates. In a lot of cases the investors will hold very large stakes of the total equity in these corporates making them important shareholders.

So how does this work? How does corporate access bring together the corporate clients and the institutional investors? Corporate access at its core is all about arranging meetings and events in which investors and corporates come together. These meetings are usually requested by the investors themselves through the research sales staff. The research sales staff will arrange these meetings with the corporates or they will have the specialized corporate access team handle this. Arranging the meeting usually involves setting up a time and venue to meet at as well as arranging for transportation or meals if needed. The meetings can vary from short meetings lasting just a couple of hours, to full on day trips where the investors visit the corporate's facilities such as factories. This gives the investors a firsthand glimpse of what is going on in the corporate that they are invested in or are considering investing in. Corporate access teams will also arrange larger more specialized events. This might entail a larger meeting where the corporate will meet with several investors at the same time and such meetings might be arranged at venues such as hotels or conference centers.

Requests for meetings might also arise from the corporate as well. This request might come in to the corporate access team from the corporate directly or through a banker in the investment banker division. The corporate might wish to set up a meeting to target a specific investor whom they would like to convince to invest in their firm.

The corporate access team will also run several investor related events during the year in the form of conferences or seminars. These events will be initiated by the broker dealer based on analysis of what the investors would like to see. Hot sectors that are attracting a lot of investor interest might form the theme of a conference that will be organized around that sector. Corporates operating in that sector will be contacted to see if they are interested in participating. Once the broker dealer has gathered together enough corporates interested in attending, it will plan out a conference. A typical conference will include public open sessions and private meetings. Public open sessions are more general topics related to the conference and a key note speaker; usually an academic or government official will be invited to speak. Conference attendees are free to attend these sessions as they like. Private meetings form the bulk of the conference time and these are simply meetings arranged between investors and corporates.

The broker dealer will invite their largest, most profitable clients first especially those who showed interest in investing in the sector.

Once the investors and corporate clients have been confirmed as attending, the team will arrange any travel plans as needed. The team will also start to book investor meetings with the corporates and arrange all the schedules for these meetings. These meeting slots are usually given out to high priority clients first based on their wishes and requests.

Finally, most conferences will start and or end with a social event such as a cocktail reception with entertainment. The corporate access team will handle all this as well dealing with the suppliers who will provide the services such as hotels, caterers and any performance artists as needed.

Corporate access much like research, is not a service that is charged for separately. It is bundled together with the commissions on trades made by the clients. Thus much like with research, corporate access is a sales tool used to create more trades. Corporate access appears on the broker review and a strong corporate access offering to clients will result in a good broker review and in turn more trading volumes from the clients.

From the corporate side there is usually no fee charged to the corporate for meetings it requests setup with investors. The hope is that by providing these services to corporates they will hopefully return to do business with the investment banking division for their capital raising and other corporate finance activities, services for which a fee will be charged.

• • •

13.2. Why are clients interested in this?

From the investor's viewpoint:

Clients are all looking for an edge in the markets and any edge that can help them increase the investment returns their end clients expect. Much the same as with other content offerings like research, corporate access offers clients another source of information and insight. Being able to meet with the management of a firm directly gives an investor a better sense of what the corporate is all about, more than just the numbers in an annual report or the words on a page in a research report could. After all, nothing can replace the sense one can get from interacting with management and getting to know more about them. Seeing and experiencing this first hand and the insights that can be gained from that experience is what investors are looking for in the corporate access content offerings at the broker dealer.

From the corporate's point of view:

Corporate access events, meetings and conferences give them a chance to connect with their current shareholders or with new ones. As noted, most of the large investment firms have large holdings especially in the largest corporations. All this assists them in managing their shareholders and keeping them happy. For the upper management of a corporation, being able to demonstrate that they can provide a return on the investor's investment ensures that when it comes time to vote on the management at the corporation the investors will back up management and support them.

Just as with managing existing investor – corporate relations; the corporate access events also help the corporates attract new investors and ensure a healthy demand for their shares. Perhaps these corporates might find themselves in a position that there is enough demand from investors that could lead to further future capital raising opportunities which the investment banking division would be happy to assist with.

Fourteen

Equity Options

14.1. What are they?

Welcome to the world of derivatives. Equity options are usually the first derivative most people are familiar with. Equity options are basically a set of contracts that gives the buyer the right but not the obligation to buy or sell the underlying asset at a certain price (known as "the strike price") on or before a specified expiry date. The seller, on the other hand, has the obligation to fulfill the transaction should the buyer of the option exercise it. The term option comes from the fact that exercising it from the point of view of the holder of the option is, well "optional"!

The seller of the option charges a premium to the buyer, which gives the buyer the right to exercise the option. The seller will keep this premium whether or not the buyer exercises the option or not. In an equity option, the underlying asset is the same basic single stock cash equity that we learned about at the start of this book, thus options are "derived" from the single stock equity that underlies them. It is also important to note that there are also options available on the other types of asset classes like bonds, interest rates and commodities, but these are topics for another book.

Equity options are traded in two main ways; either on the market or off the market. Options traded on the market are also known by the terms; "exchange traded options", "listed options" or "vanilla options". These feature a standardized set of deliverables in terms of quality, quantity and time to expiry which are defined by the exchange on which they trade. Usually the exchange sets standardized contract sizes of 100 shares, the prices are also standardized in specified increments as are the expiry dates. In U.S. markets, exchange traded equity options expire on the third Saturday of the month which means that the third Friday is a heavy day of activity. Finally, exchange traded options, much like cash equity trades, are settled through a clearing house and the fulfillment of the trade is guaranteed.

The other type of equity option trade is known as an over the counter trade or an "OTC trade". These are also called "exotic options" or just "exotics". OTC trades are specific customizable trades done between two parties; in which the terms and conditions are fully determined by the two parties to the contract. This means that the price, size and expiry date of the option are completely customizable to whatever the two parties agree to. However, since they are not standardized and they are not conducted on an exchange there is the risk that one party might default on the terms of the option should it become exercisable. Usually OTC options are conducted between two large institutions and the broker dealers are heavily involved in this space offering customized solutions to clients.

Regardless of whether an option is exchange traded or OTC traded, there are two main types of equity option available, the call option and the put option. They are the opposite of each other but regardless of whether it is a call or put option the buyer of the option will need to pay a premium to seller or the writer of the option as already noted. The option premium is the cost of the derivative. A call option allows the buyer the right to buy stock from the seller at the strike price agreed to during the time period the option lasts for. The strategy of a call option is that the buyer can secure a price to buy at and hopes that the stock price will rise and thus use the option to buy the stock at a lower price and turn around and sell it at a higher price.

A put option allows the buyer the right to sell a stock to the seller of the option at a strike price agreed to during the time period that the option lasts for. The idea with a put option is that the buyer can secure a sell price and hopes that the price will decline in value allowing him to buy the stock and turn around and sell it at the higher agreed to price and make a profit.

As noted for both call and put options, it costs money to get into these contracts and that is known as the "premium" which varies in price. Let's look at what influences the option's premiums and then later on, the key factors that come into play as to whether or not an option gets exercised.

The price of underlying single stock is the single most influential factor in the premium for an option. As the price of the underlying equity increases, premiums for call options increase and those for put options decrease. Conversely, as the price of the underlying equity decreases the opposite happens, the premiums for call options decrease and those for put options increase. The price volatility of the underlying stock also impacts the price of the premium. The more volatile the underlying equity is based on historical price movements, the greater the chance that the option could move into the money allowing it to be exercised and thus the higher the premium. Conversely, more stable historical price movements in the underlying reduce the premium.

The risk free interest rate also affects the price of the option. The risk free interest rate is the interest return you can expect on your money without taking any risk. This is considered as the interest rate you would receive on government bonds and treasury bills which are considered the most risk free assets available because the government can always raise taxes to pay the interest owed on government bonds or treasury bills whereas other borrowers like corporations do not have that unique power. As the risk free interest rate rises, the premiums on call options will increase and those on put options will decrease and vice versa. The reason for this is that the risk free interest rate reflects the opportunity cost of capital. When interest rates are high it is less attractive to buy stocks because why buy a stock with its risk of price fluctuations when you have a nice safe government bond available. Buying options are cheaper per share than buying the underlying securities. Options allow you to control the more shares but at a far lower cost of capital. Thus in times of high interest rates, call options become more desirable because they do not cost as much capital leaving the investors able to invest that capital in those nice safe government bonds. Increased demand for call options like anything in life leads to increased prices. With put options the interest rate has a slightly different effect but it still reflects the opportunity cost of capital. A put allows you to sell shares at a certain price and are best used when stock prices are declining. In a declining market another option is to sell shares short. Thus a put is seen in the same light as a short sale. When you short sell a stock you receive the cash and of course have to buy the stock back later. In times of high interest rates it is better to short sell a stock and receive the cash from the sale and invest it in a risk free government bond. Why buy a put option which costs you capital when you can short sell and receive capital and invest that until you have to use some of it to buy the stock back. Thus the demand for put options is less in high interest rate time periods.

Finally, dividends on the underlying stock that the option is based on will have an impact on the price of the premium. For call options, an increase in the dividend payout on the underlying stock reduces the price of the call options and increases the price of the put prices and vice versa. The reason for this is that a dividend is paid to the holders of the underlying stock but the call option holders get nothing. This makes owning the underlying stock more attractive than the option and thus the demand for the option goes down and so does the price of the premium. If the opposite where true and the dividend payout was cut on the underlying then there is less attraction in holding the stock compared to the option and the option premium will increase.

For put options the opposite is true. A raising dividend increases the price of the put and a falling dividend decreases it. The reason for this is again tied to the selling the stock short compared to buying a put option. If you recall from the section on securities lending, when stocks are borrowed the dividends must be repaid to the party you borrowed the stock from. Well an increase in dividend means more to pay back to the lender for short sales so the put option appears more attractive as an alternative and thus its price increases.

Tied in with all these factors that affect the price of the option premium are the concepts of intrinsic value and time value that determine the value of the option. Intrinsic value is the real value of an option at a given point in time; the amount that you can expect to receive if you were to exercise the option. Intrinsic value only occurs when the option is actually exercisable for a profit. The strike price and the underlying price determine if the option has any intrinsic value. Intrinsic value is the difference between the underlying price of the single stock equity and the strike price of the option contract. The intrinsic value can be described as follows depending on the type of option:

For a call option: intrinsic value = the underlying price – the strike price
For a put option: intrinsic value = the strike price – the underlying price

The intrinsic value for an option only arises when the options are "in the money" which means that the buyer can possibly exercise them for profit which differs depending on whether the option is a put or a call. Options out of the money cannot be exercised and thus there is no intrinsic value to them. Options are in or out of the money as follows:

For a call option:
- in the money: the strike price < the underlying price
- out of the money: the strike price > the underlying price
- at the money: the strike price = the underlying price

For a put option:
- in the money: the strike price > the underlying price
- out of the money: the strike price < the underlying price
- at the money: the strike price = the underlying price

For example, if a stock is trading at $10 and there is a call option available in the option market with a strike price of $8.00 with 1 month left until expiry and the premium was $2.50 the intrinsic value would be:

For a call option: the underlying price ($10.00) – the strike price ($8.00) = intrinsic value ($2.00)

That $2.00 represents the minimum value you can expect from exercising the option. If the option was at the money or out of the money there would be no intrinsic value as it would not be profitable to exercise it. Thus at the money and out of the money options have no intrinsic value to them.

Now we need to look at the time value (also sometimes referred to as "extrinsic value") which is related to intrinsic value and also by extension to being "in the money" or "out of the money". Time value is the amount by which the price of the option exceeds the intrinsic value. The calculation of time value is the same for both put and call options and is as follows:

Time value = premium (call or put option) – intrinsic value.

So for our call option example above the time value or extrinsic value is:

premium ($2.50) – intrinsic value ($2.00) = time value ($0.50)

An option that is not in the money only consists of time value as there is no real value, nothing intrinsic in terms of profit that could be had. All you have is time with the hope that the underlying price moves enough so that you as the option holder can exercise the option and make a profit. As the option approaches expiry the time value will start to decline and this speeds up as it approaches expiry. This basically reflects the fact that there is less time before expiry for the price to move to either put the option in the money if it is not already or to put it further into the money.

So we have covered the basics about what an option is, where they are traded, what types of options are available, how the premiums for them are priced, the concepts of intrinsic / extrinsic value and the concept of being in / out / at the money. Let's look at the call option and put option in detail with an example that will tie all this together starting with the call option first.

With a call option, the buyer of the option has the right but not the obligation to buy an agreed on quantity of shares of the underlying equity. The seller of the option, also known as the "writer," on the other hand agrees to sell them to the buyer at or before a certain time as long as a strike price has been met. The buyer pays the seller the premium on a per-share basis for this right.

The stock ABC Incorporated is currently trading at $20.50 a share. Analysts at the broker dealer feel it is going to go much higher in the next three months, probably to around $26-$27 a share. One of the research sales staff reads this research because he knows that one of his big clients is interested in taking a position in ABC Incorporated.

He thinks that his client might be interested in using an option to gain exposure, so he checks the options market by talking to a trader on the derivatives desk with whom he consults as he develops this trade idea. He finds sellers offering call options at a price of $22.00 (the strike price) which will expire in three months time with a premium of $2.00 a share. He calls his clients and pitches the trading idea to buy options and use them to hopefully make a profit.

This option is currently out of the money and has no intrinsic value but the client trusts the analyst to be correct as he has in the past and agrees to buy an option for 100 shares on ABC Incorporated (the underlying) paying a premium of $200 ($2.00 a share on 100 shares) to the seller or writer of the option. The seller is now obligated to sell the shares at $22.00 a share should the buyer exercise the contract within the next three months. If the buyer does not exercise the contract in the next three months the seller keeps the shares and the $200.00 premium.

The seller, the research salesperson, and his client who bought the call option all watch the stock price of ABC over the next three months as it is now the sole driver of what will happen with the option. A week after the seller sold the option the share price on ABC Incorporated declines to $19.50 and the option is now really "out of the money" with the price of the underlying below the strike price. The seller is happy and as long as the price stays below $22.00 a share and "out of the money," he can keep the shares and made $200 in profit from the premium the buyer paid.

A month has passed since the option was first bought and now the share price is $22.00 which makes it "at the money" as the strike price equals the underlying price and now the client could exercise the option to buy the shares from the seller and the seller is obligated to sell. However, the client can buy the shares in the open market for the same price instead of having to use the option so the option still has no intrinsic value as we can see in the following calculation:

underlying price ($22.00) – the strike price ($22.00) = intrinsic value ($0.00). The client holds on to the option as it still has two months left and there is no point in using it now.

Another month passes and the price is now $24.00 a share with one month left until expiry. The option is still "in the money" as the strike price was $22.00. The strike price is less than the underlying now and we have intrinsic value of $2.00 a share as follows: the underlying price ($24.00) – the strike price ($22.00) = intrinsic value ($2.00). However, the client is still not going to make any money as they had to pay $2.00 a share as a premium on the option so the client is only just going to break even so they hold off exercising it. Of course the goal is to make a profit and with one month left on the option the client is going to wait. It is important to note that the premium for this option would have increased in the market as it is now in the money and anyone buying this same option now that the client bought 2 months ago would pay a higher premium.

Two weeks later the price suddenly starts to go up and hits $27.00 a share just as the analyst was predicting. The client chooses to exercise the option and "call" away the 100 shares from the seller paying the seller the strike price of $22.00 a share for 100 shares for a total of $2,200 making their total cost $2,400 considering the $200 premium already paid. The client takes possession of the shares from the seller of the option and then instructs the broker dealer to sell the 100 shares at $27.00 a share for a total of $2,700 making a profit of $300. The client could have potentially waited another two weeks as the option still had two weeks to go until expiry and waited to see if the price of the underlying increased further but instead of taking the risk that the price could drop they exercised the option and took their profits.

Instead of exercising the option the client could have simply sold the option contracts. Now that the option is in the money the contracts have become worth more because why would the client sell a contract for $2.00 to allow the buyer to buy shares at $22.00 when the price is already $27.00 and the buyer is guaranteed a profit of at least $3.00 a share ($27.00 - $22.00 - $2.00 for the premium). Prices of the option contract will move up as the option moves more and more into the money. The price of the option contract should be around $5.00 now considering that the price of the underlying is $5.00 over the strike price. In reality, when taking profits on option trades most are sold when the price of the option rises above what was paid for it as opposed to exercising the option and then selling the stock.

This is how a call option is used to potentially make money. However, the price of the underlying could have stayed below the strike price of the option (or at least below the breakeven price to the client) for the whole three months and the option could have expired without ever being used. In that case the seller keeps the shares and of course the premium paid.

The put option works much the same but in reverse. A put option gives the buyer the right to sell the underlying but not the obligation to sell. The seller or writer of the put option is obligated to buy the shares if the put option is exercised by the buyer and receives a premium for this from the buyer. Just as with a call option; the seller of the put option keeps the premium regardless of what happens.

The client feels that a certain stock; XYZ Corporation will fall in the near term and wants to take advantage of this fall in price. They discuss this with the broker dealer and look for some short term trading ideas involving options. The client decides to buy a put option on XYZ Corporation. The current price of XYZ Corporation is $20.00 a share. The client buys a put option for 100 shares on XYZ Corporation from the put seller (writer) for a premium of $1.50 a share for a total cost of $150.00. The strike price for this put option is $18.00 and the expiry is 3 months away.

Notice how the strike price is lower than the current market price which is opposite from the call option case.

Over the next three months the client (as buyer) and the option seller watch the stock price. The price falls to $17.00 a share and now the option is in the money and has intrinsic value. The client can buy the shares on the market at $17.00 a share and force the seller of the option to buy them from him at $18.00 a share which is the strike price and make $100.00 doing so. However, the client will not break-even as they paid the option writer $150.00 for the put as a premium. Just like with the call option above, the premium plays a role in determining how profitable an option will be. So the client waits a couple of weeks and things change when the stock price falls to $13.00. Now the client exercises the put option and buys 100 shares at $13.00 for a total of $1,300 in the open market and the seller of the put option has to buy the shares at the strike price of $18.00 as agreed to. The client who bought the option thus sells the shares to the seller (writer) of the option at $1,800 and makes $500 on the difference less the $150 initial premium for a total profit of $350. Just as with a call option, the client could simply have sold the option contract as its price would have increased the more it moved into the money instead of actually exercising the option. The result would have been the same; the client would have made money speculating that the market price of XYZ was going to fall.

There are several different types of exercisability available with put and call options. American options allow the buyer to exercise the option at any time between the date of purchase and the date of expiry. The two examples above are both based American options. European options are only exercisable at the date of expiry making them the most restrictive type of option. Bermudan options are only exercisable on certain dates before the expiry date, for example, once a week on Friday until they expire. Asian options are those that have their payout determined by the average price of the underlying equity over some preset time period. It is important to note that these names have nothing to do with geography and you can find the various option types on any exchange in any part of the world.

Aside from equity options on single stock, there are also equity options on an equity index. These are options that function the same as their single stock cousins we covered above but the difference is that the underlying is based on the index as a whole and the index is in turn based on all the values of all the single stocks within it. Just like with an option based on a single stock; as the price of the underlying equity index increases, premiums for call options increase and those for put options decrease. Conversely, as the price of the underlying equity index decreases the opposite happens, the premiums for call options decrease and those for put options increase. The same factors that influence the price of the single stock option influence the equity index option and the concepts of time value and intrinsic value are just as relevant.

There are, however, some key differences to note about index options versus single stock options. Strike prices and premiums are usually quoted in points just like the index itself is quoted in points. In order to covert this in to a monetary amount a multiplier is applied and this varies from index to index. For example the multiplier might be $100 per point (generally $100 per point is used) and an equity index option with a premium of 10 points would cost $1,000. The biggest difference in how these options work is that there is no stock involved. If the option is exercised there is no stock to deliver like there would be in the single stock option. Instead if you exercise an option you receive cash.

For example, for an equity index call option with the index value above the strike price (which means that the option is in the money) the buyer of this option can elect to exercise the option and receive the cash amount which is calculated as the difference between the strike price and the level of the underlying index. Let's say that the index is worth 100.00 points now and the call option for the index has a strike price of 80.00. The buyer of the call option contract would receive: (100 – 80) * $100 for a total of $2,000 which the seller of the index option pays to the buyer. Also, let's assume that the premium the buyer paid was 10 points at $100 a point when the option was first bought so that means the premium would have been $1,000. In the end, the buyer of the index option earns $1,000 in profit after exercising it.

With a put option it works much the same but only if the underlying index is below the strike price. So let's assume that the buyer bought an index put option for a premium of 10 points ($1,000) with a strike price of 80 and the index is currently at 60. The difference is 20 points which is $2,000 the seller must pay to the buyer and after the premium is considered the buyer makes $1,000 in profit.

It is important to note that for all exchange traded options, single stock and or equity index, the broker dealer will charge the client a commission fee per contract for doing this just like they would with any other product that we have covered so far. We have left this out of the examples to keep it simple but that commission fee would also have to be considered when it comes to making sure that the option is in the money enough to cover the premium paid and any commissions to the broker or other fees.

For OTC options which are highly customized, the broker dealer might enter into the option contract with the client and act as counterparty to the trade. In this case there is no commission fee taken but the broker dealer will price the option offered to the client in such a manner so as to give the broker dealer a greater chance to make a profit on the trade.

• • •

14.2. Why do clients buy this product?

Hedging:

Options can be used as a hedge against a movement in the price of the underlying security. For example, a client sold some shares short and in order to protect against a rise in the price of those shares (remember, with a short sell you are expecting the price to decline) they can use a call option. Should the share price rise they can call away the shares and use those shares to close out the short position. This can help short sellers guard against the risk of a price increase in the stock that they sold short.

A put option, on the other hand, helps to protect against a decline in the price of a stock and hedges against that risk. In an uncertain market where the prices of stocks are expected to decline, a portfolio manager may buy puts on some of the stocks in his portfolio that he thinks are going to decline a lot. Buying these put options allows the portfolio manager to sell the stock at the strike price of the put. If the market price falls, the portfolio manager exercises the put options and sells them at the strike price instead of at the lower market price. A put can be considered a form of insurance and should you not be able to exercise the put -because the price never moves low enough- then all that is lost is the price of the premium.

Leverage:

Another good use of options is that you can leverage your purchasing power. If a portfolio manager is considering investing $100,000 in a stock that is worth $10 a share he can buy 10,000 shares (ignoring commission and fees). However, he can control the same number of shares by buying a call option. If there are option contracts available in the market for $1 a share (or a total of $100 for a single option contact which contains 100 shares, the standard contract size) then it would cost just $10,000 (again ignoring commissions and fees) to buy 100 options contacts to control those same 10,000 shares. Leveraging in this example allows the portfolio manager to leverage his position up to a factor of 10; for every $10,000, the stock buyer can buy 1,000 shares, for the same $10,000, the options buyer can buy contracts to control 10,000 shares, 10 times the amount of the stock buyer.

Let's look at a scenario which highlights the leverage that options can provide. One portfolio manager just bought 100,000 shares at $10 each for a total cost of $1,000,000 (again ignoring commissions and fees). Another portfolio manager bought 1,000 call option contracts at a premium of $1.00 a share meaning each contact for 100 shares cost $100.00. The total cost is thus $100,000 and gives him control of the same 100,000 shares. Two weeks later, the price of the underlying increases to $12.50 a share. The portfolio manager who bought the shares sells them for $1,250,000 and earns $250,000 which is a return of 25% on his initial investment of $1,000,000.

The portfolio manager who bought the options sells his 1,000 option contracts now valued at around at least $2.50 per share ($250 for a contact of 100 shares) for a total of $250,000. He had to pay $100,000 as a premium so that leaves him with $150,000 in profit which is less than that of the other portfolio manager but here is the real power of leverage, the portfolio manager who bought the options only had to invest $100,000 and received $250,000 and $150,000 in profit at the end. This is a return of 150% which is far more than the 25% that the other portfolio manager made. Sure the overall profit in dollar terms is less for the option user but the option user made a far more effective use of capital in terms of return. It is important to note that while options offer leverage, the portfolio manager who bought the options could have lost the entire amount of the $100,000 premium if the stock price never moved enough before it expired to make the option worth using. Meanwhile, the portfolio manager who bought the stock would still have the stock as an asset and would hopefully be able to sell it for a higher price later on.

Fifteen

Structured Derivatives

15.1. What are they?

Structured derivatives are a highly specialized area within the broker dealer. Unlike with cash equities, programs or with options there is no one clear product that a structuring team will deal with. Structuring can potentially involve any number or combination of products. The structuring team essentially offers two types of products to clients, standard prepackaged structured products and bespoke (customized) products.

With a standard prepackaged structured product, a base investment strategy is determined for the product and the return on this is usually linked to the performance of an underlying security. In case of equities, it could be a single stock, a collection of stocks or, perhaps an entire stock market index. Structured products can be based on other underlying securities such as bonds and commodities or even foreign exchange as well. Combinations of different asset classes such as mixing bonds and stock together are possible. The work of the team involved might bleed over into other products so this is not just an equity product like all the others we have covered so far. Most of the prepackaged structured products involve the use of derivative products like futures or options as well as other complex combinations. A lot of these structured products feature guarantees around the principal invested by the client which means that the client cannot lose their principle or a portion of the principle they invested.

Let's take a look at an example of a prepackaged structured derivative known as an Equity Linked Note to get an idea what this is all about. In spite of the name including the word "equity", the product is actually classified as a bond or fixed income security but it is linked to the return of an underlying equity index. This is an example of what we were talking about with structured products bleeding over into other product areas outside of just equities. The product is generally composed of a debt instrument combined with a call option and as we learned, the value of the option is tied to some underlying equity or perhaps an equity index. The structuring team issues a zero coupon bond which is a bond that does not pay interest but at maturity will pay out at a higher price. You can think of it as buying a bond now at $90.00 and then when it matures you will receive $100.00. Just for comparisons sake, a normal bond would have been bought at $100.00 and it will pay interest until it matures. When it matures, the amount that you will receive is $100.00, the amount that you initially invested.

The structuring team at the broker dealer is responsible for the bond as issuer and will guarantee the repayment of the principle; usually between 80% - 100% depending on terms of the product. Thus this product provides protection of the principle in the form of a bond and allows the client to participate in the appreciation of the price of the underlying equity (assuming it appreciates of course). Should the equity linked note not appreciate then the principle will be returned to the client at whatever percentage was agreed on. Much like a bond, an equity linked note has a maturity date. The payout at maturity is determined by the level of the underlying equity that the option is linked to. Just like with an option, the equity linked note contains a "strike price". The option within the note will determine the end result and if the payoff is profitable or not. If the price of the underlying equity is above the strike price, then the equity linked note will have been profitable for the investor. If the price of the underlying is below the strike price, then the note will just return the principle invested. However, unlike with an option were the option holder can sometimes exercise the option at any time before expiry (like with an American option) this is not available with equity linked notes and the payout is only determined at maturity.

Should the note end up being profitable to the owner, the final payout will be influenced by a final factor called the participation rate. The participation rate is the amount of the appreciation of the underlying equity that the investor gets to enjoy. It will vary between notes and the issuers of the notes. For example, if the participation rate is 100% then the full amount that the equity appreciates will be considered in the payout. If the rate was only 75% then only 75% of the gain will be paid out to the owner.

Let's look at two examples to get an idea as to how this works. There are two equity linked notes being issued on ABC Corporation by the broker dealer's structuring team. Both have maturities of one year and face values of $100,000 and the strike price of ABC stock is $10.00. One has the principle guaranteed at 75% with a 100% participation rate. The other has the principle guaranteed at 100% but only a 75% participation rate. The sales team sells one note each to two different clients. One year from now the notes mature and the price of ABC corporation while it had many ups and down over the year is at $12.00 a share; an increase of 20%. Client A with the 100% participation rate note will receive: 100% (participation rate) * 20% (the appreciation amount) * $100,000 (the principle) for a total profit $20,000 and a total payout of $120,000 including the original $100,000 investment. Client B with the 75% participation note will receive: 75% (participation rate) * 20% (the appreciation amount) * $100,000 (the principle) for a total profit of: $15,000 and a total payout of $115,000 including the original $100,000 investment. However, should the stock price be less than $10.00 client A would only receive $75,000 back as only 75% of the principle was guaranteed whereas client B would have received $100,000 in principle back as the full value of the note was covered. It is important to note that should the issuer go bankrupt before the note matures the whole concept of "guaranteed principle" does not apply anymore, thus equity linked notes have a counterparty risk factor to consider when they are bought.

When the client discusses the equity linked note with the broker dealer they will be able to customize it somewhat and determine what the underlying equity will be (a single stock, a basket or equity or perhaps an equity index), the maturity date they want and the amount to invest. The prepackaged parts are the concept of using the zero coupon bond together with the use of the call option. Aside from equity linked notes, there are other prepackaged structured products available such as an equity linked foreign exchange option, which is a currency option paired with an equity forward contract. There are a variety of prepackaged options available for clients to invest in.

The other type of structured product available is the bespoke or customized structured derivative. There are no set products or combinations of products like that we see with the equity linked note. Indeed there could be any combination of derivatives used together with other equity products or non equity products.

Clients are usually interested in using a bespoke structured derivative to solve a particular business issue that they face such as a tax or financing problem. The structuring team will try to come up with solutions to the problem however, the client themselves may not know exactly what they want to achieve and perhaps only have vague ideas about it. This means constant communication with the client as the plan is developed taking the client's input along the way and breaking it down into a financial solution which provides a "structure" to resolve the issue in.

When dealing with bespoke structuring there are often a lot of legal and tax issues that the client will have to face and the structuring team will take these into consideration when working on the solution. There are a lot of potential issues to consider and in some cases the client is not just looking for a new investing idea designed to make money but they may well be more concerned with tax or accounting issues. Affects on the client's balance sheet would also have to be considered as well especially with complex transactions.

The broker dealer will charge a client for these products and the pricing of them is a big concern especially for complex multi stage transactions. The fee will usually be priced into the structured solution and it may not be explicit like a basis point fee on a single stock equity trade.

• • •

15.2. Why do clients buy this product?

Portfolio diversification:

As noted, these products can offer a client an alternative to investing in regular equities or even the basic derivatives like options. These products can be customized to give the client access to different investment avenues all over the world exposing the client to assets that they might not otherwise be able to access. The client can also customize the returns to be based on an underlying product that the client desires. All this can be available with some form of capital protection built in depending on the product.

Customizable:

Structuring is the one product that can be customized to meet a client's needs. Regular listed products like options, futures or, stocks themselves, are available as is. The broker dealer can provide clients with a customized set of solutions to take advantage of a particular market scenario, to provide the client with leverage as needed or to take care of a legal or accounting issue. At the end of the day, structuring usually comes down to the transfer of risk from one party to another and the flexible, albeit complex nature of a structured derivative allows the clients to do this.

Sixteen
Delta One

16.1. What is it?

Delta One is not really a product in and of its own but it is an umbrella term that consists of a variety of different products and the exact content of what a Delta One desk will deal with will differ from bank to bank. Delta One is mainly concerned with derivatives and indeed the name "Delta One" refers to the "delta" which measures the change in the price of a derivative compared to the change in the price of the underlying. The "delta" is one of "the Greeks', which are a set of measures (named because they are represented by Greek letters) designed to measure how sensitive the value of an asset is to changes in underlying parameters such as the price, volatility and time to expiry etc. The Greeks measure various dimensions of risk and are an important part of derivative valuation and risk management. There are quite a few Greeks to learn about but that is a topic for another book. Since the scope of this book is to provide an introduction to the broker dealer and the products and services it sells, we have left them out but it is important to note them as the reader will encounter them if they delve into more specific products. The Delta One desk is named after one of the measures and the term "One" means that for a given percentage move in the price of the underlying stock there will be a nearly identical move; a one to one correlation in the price of the derivative. Of course this is just a name and all Delta One products do not always have this characteristic all the time.

Delta One as a product group usually covers futures, forwards, ETFs, transition management, index arbitrage and swaps. Delta One will also combine with other products like single stocks, algorithm trading and options that we have already covered. There is a wide range of trading activities that this desk undertakes with clients. In this section we are going to look at transition management, ETFs and index arbitrage in some detail and we will cover futures, forwards and swaps in their own sections that will follow on after this.

Let's start with transition management. Transition management is a service in which the broker dealer helps clients buy or sell large volumes of various stocks because the client might be transitioning from one set of holdings to another. An example of this might apply to a client that manages a large set of index funds. Index funds are designed to be passive investment vehicles that track the performance of the index. The fund itself is constructed of the same component individual single stocks that make up the index and in the same proportion. These indices change from time to time as the stocks in them change due to corporate mergers, bankruptcies and other changes. When an index changes, the portfolio managers at the client have to change the composition of their index funds to match the changes in the index, buying and selling large holdings in a short period of time. In other cases perhaps the portfolio manager might want to shut down a fund that is not popular so they have to liquidate the holdings. Management changes within the client could cause a new portfolio manager to come to manage a fund and he or she might want to make changes to the fund's composition and thus large numbers of securities might need to be bought or sold.

These large orders are known as "transition management" and the broker dealer's Delta One desk will handle this. Sometimes, depending on the broker dealer, transition management might be part of the programs desk. A large transitional management order will be shopped around to see which broker dealer can offer the best prices in terms of commission as well as being able to handle the order in such a way that the transition can happen without disturbing the market. After all, a large number of large sell or buy orders will really move supply and demand causing sudden price movements and affect the prices that the portfolio manager will have to pay or will get for his securities. The broker dealer is expected to have the execution expertise to minimize this.

ETFs are another area that the Delta One desk will deal with. We have already covered ETFs in a previous section however the way the Delta One desk deals with them is a further extension on this. Remember when we spoke about creation units? Well the Delta One desk is usually the area of the broker dealer who is involved with those creation units as an "authorized participant". The desk will function as a market maker for the ETF and as we know this means that they list up prices and are ready to buy and sell ETF units as needed and they make money on the spread between the bid and ask prices. This could mean selling ETF units from its existing inventory or buying them in the market as needed.

As part of this market making activity, Delta One desk is also involved with the creation unit aspect as the broker dealer is an "authorized participant". The desk can buy up the individual stocks that make up one (or more) creation units for a particular ETF and sell them to the ETF issuer in return for ETF units or the desk can take ETF units and get the creation units and the shares that they contain from the issuer in return. An ETF contains a lot of "moving parts" within it in the form of all the individual stocks that collectively make up the ETF. The individual prices of all these stocks change throughout the day leading to cases were the price of the ETF does not match up with the total price of all the individual stocks that make it up. This creates an opportunity for price arbitrage. Arbitrage is all about buying an asset at a lower price and being able to sell it somewhere else like on a different market or in a different form for a higher price. The Delta One desk will try to convert creation units to ETF units and vice versa to take advantage and arbitrage these price differences to make a profit. For example, if the ETF is cheaper than the underlying shares within it, the desk will buy up enough ETF units equal to one creation unit and redeem that creation unit for the underlying stocks and then turn around and sell those individual stocks on the market and make a profit on the price difference. Conversely, if the ETF is more expensive than the underlying shares that make up the ETF, the desk can buy the individual stocks and deliver them as a creation unit to receive the ETF units in exchange which the desk will then turn around and sell these higher priced ETF units in the market. This change of form from individual shares to ETFs and back again is what is at the heart of this type of arbitrage.

These arbitrage opportunities usually only last a short time because other market participants including other broker dealers are watching for them as well. Thus arbitrage is done in conjunction with algorithms that can find these price differences and trade on them quickly. The number of shares involved is also large because the individual price differences on the shares is usually very small and only trading in a large number of shares will make it profitable especially when the costs to make these trades are taken into consideration.

The Delta One desk is also involved in another type of ETF activity and that is creating ETFs that are synthetic and may not actually hold any individual shares in them. An example of this is when the broker dealer gives cash not securities for a creation unit to the ETF issuer. The ETF issuer gives creation units to the broker dealer's Delta One desk and the desk can sell these in the market. There are many other ways that ETFs can be created out of derivatives and these are all covered by the Delta One desk.

Index Arbitrage is the final product that we will cover in this section. We have already spoken of the concept of arbitrage with

ETFs and index arbitrage is no different as the index, much like the ETFs that track it, is full of stocks with constant price changes. At its core, index arbitrage is a strategy looking to exploit small discrepancies between the prices of stocks that comprise an index compared to the price of a futures contract on that index. While we have not yet covered futures (they will be covered in the following section) we can still use this product as an introduction to the concept.

The price differences between the index and the futures contract will only exist for a short time as market participants will find these price differences and quickly exploit them just like with arbitrage on ETFs. Therefore, it is important to buy or sell the two products at the same time and the use of algorithmic trading techniques is necessary in getting these orders to the market as quickly as possible and trading them all at the same time.

In addition to the main products covered above, Delta One is also home to more exotic and specialized products such as; option synthetics and reverse conversions, repos and various other arbitrage strategies. These products can be very complex and there is no limit to what the Delta One desk can create. So how does this product category make money for the broker dealer?

The Delta One desk makes money on all of these products in the spreads between how much it sells them to the clients for versus and how much they can source them for in the market. In addition, the traders on the desk will hedge the trades they make with the client counterparties by hedging with the broker dealer's own money. These hedges are done with other counterparties such as other broker dealers or even with other clients. These hedges while designed to manage risk and limit loss, can also result in some profits if the risk is played out right. Regardless, all the activities of the desk result in a complex series of trades of various types amongst a wide variety of counterparties which means that while there is a lot of opportunity for the broker dealer to earn a profit, there is also a lot of risk to be managed. This risk has attracted some concerns from regulators in recent years.

After the financial crisis of 2008, some jurisdictions especially in the United States as seen with the Volcker rule, banned broker dealers from trading with their own capital. This rule prevents broker dealers from using their own capital and trying to make a profit in what is known as proprietary trading (which we will look at in the last section of this book). However, the Delta One desk sometimes uses its own capital in transactions, facilitating client trades by acting as counterparty, or in hedging activities resulting from trades with clients. In these cases it is hard to know what trades are for clients or with clients and what trades are purely proprietary trades made only for the broker dealer and do not involve any clients. This is still an area of controversy within the broker dealer industry.

• • •

16.2. Why do clients buy this product?

Opportunities:

Clients will deal with the Delta One desk and the group of products offered simply because it offers them more varied ways to potentially earn profits. Large institutional investors, like the type that we are focusing on in this book, have the capital available to take advantage of this. More options to trade and more options to hedge various positions appeal to the clients who, like always, are looking for enhanced returns on their investing capital.

Customized Client Solutions:

Much like with structured derivatives, Delta one gives the clients options to create more customized solutions to their investment needs and potentially achieve higher returns on their investment capital. The one difference is that with structured derivatives, tax and legal concerns are usually important drivers. With Delta One, the main drivers are usually risk related; such as managing the impact of large transactions in the market like those that would take place with transition management.

Seventeen

Equity Futures and Forwards

17.1. What are they?

Futures and forwards are another form of derivative just like the options we looked at previously. You may have heard of them in the financial media with comments like "the price of pork belly futures....". Futures and forwards initially started off as financial instruments used to help farmers set prices on agricultural products like rice, wheat and those delicious pork bellies. Like all financial products, they have developed a lot from their roots and now they are available for both single stock equities and also on equity indexes. So how does this all work then?

At their core they are a contractual agreement between two parties to buy and sell a specified product (the underlying that the future or forward is based on) with a standardized quantity that is to be delivered in the future for a price which is determined today. Let's take a look at an example about how this historically came about with agricultural products.

Farmers would bring their crops to market at harvest time and then try to sell them. Sometimes the prices would be high depending on demand and sometimes the farmer would not be able to sell all his crops if demand was low or if there was lot of supply in the market. Forwards initially developed to help both producers and buyers ensure more stable prices and supplies. You can see how this would be useful to farmers who could plan ahead and reserve a price today for a product that they are going to have to sell in the future anyway. The term "forward" came from the "forward looking" price that was being discussed at that time the contracts were made.

From the farmer's point of view he was happy to be able to secure a price for his crop or livestock ahead of time. From the buyer's point of view (such as a baker making bread with the wheat the farmer grew, or a butcher making bacon with those delicious pork bellies) they were happy to know how much they were going to get and at what price. Forwards helped both buyers and sellers determine prices and supply in terms of the quantity to be delivered. A farmer would sell a forward contract for a crop that was still growing in the fields or livestock he was still raising. These products would be ready for delivery in a few months time to a buyer at a price agreed on now. The buyer would be considered "long" as the buyer will take possession of the product at a future date and become the ultimate owner. The farmer selling the contract is considered to be "short" because he owes the buyer the crop at a future date and is not the ultimate owner as he has sold it. Being "long" means that you will benefit from an increase in price as you have bought the asset now while it was cheaper. Being "short" means that you will benefit from a decline in price as you have sold the asset now at a higher price than you would be able to get in the future. When applied to a forward contract for a single stock the buyer of the contract agrees to take delivery of the shares in the future thus the buyer hopes that the price will increase as he will be able to receive the shares as the price he paid when the contract was first signed which would be cheaper than the price when he takes delivery. The seller of the single stock contract hopes that the price will decline which means that he would have sold them at the start of the contract at a higher price than he has to deliver them at. In any forward or futures contract there is always one party that is "short" and one that is "long". Unlike with short selling a stock were you have to borrow the stock now and repay it later; there is no such need to borrow anything when being short in a equity forward or futures contract and it is just as easy to be short with an equity forward or future as it is to be long.

Both forwards and futures look like they are the same thing as both are concerned about a contract with an agreed to future price to deliver a certain single stock or equity index. Well, what is the difference between these two products then?

First of all a futures contract is traded on an exchange. All the contracts are standardized and set for standardized amounts usually one futures contract for a single stock would represent 100 underlying shares. For equity index futures the contracts work a little differently. They do not represent any amount of shares but rather they represent the index value and each point movement change in the value of the index represents a price movement of a certain amount. There are various "sizes" in terms of how much a point movement is worth. For the exchange traded futures contracts there is a clearing house, which like with single stock equity trades, acts as a counterparty to both parties to the futures contract and ensures that each side receives what is expected. Both parties to the contract are required to put up a minimal amount which covers a portion of the full value of the contract at the start. This is known as the margin amount. Futures contract values are marked to market everyday which means that gains and losses in contract value are compared between the two parties and an exchange of those gains and losses are made daily. Thus market participants might have to contribute more to the initial margin amount to cover losses and likewise they may have surpluses above the margin amount they initially deposited when they have gains. We will cover this process in more detail soon.

For a forward contract there is no exchange to trade them on. These are fully OTC (over the counter) trades and each contract is separate and customized to whatever terms the two parties agree to and this can include multiple products mixed in including, but not limited to, equity products. There is no clearing house and thus the parties to the trade are at risk that the other counterparty might default on their forward agreement. The broker dealer will usually act as counterparty to an agreement with a client to meet whatever the client's needs are. There is no marking to market and any exchange of payments as there are with a futures contract, payments only take place at the end of the contract once it matures. Likewise, since the contracts are customized and there is no exchange to trade them on, there is no easy way to end the contract before maturity and thus most forward contracts are held to maturity. The contracts can be terminated early but the counterparty wishing to terminate it will have to find another counterparty and conduct an exact opposite contract with them. Forward contracts are not as regulated because they are customized "private" contracts; futures contracts on the other hand are more closely regulated by various government agencies.

Now that we have seen the difference between forwards and futures we want to take a quick look at how they compare to options as there can be some confusion between these products sometimes. With both forwards, futures and options you are concerned with the future price of the underlying and one party has to deliver something to the other however there are some key differences. The most important difference occurs in the obligations that each product brings. Options, if we recall, give the buyer the option to exercise the contract and there is no requirement to do so. The option seller only has to deliver if the option is exercised. With a forward or futures contract, both parties have obligations to fulfill; the buyer has to buy at the price agreed to and the seller has sell the underlying. With an option, the buyer pays a premium for the right to exercise the option if the buyer wants to at a future date and there is no obligation to do so. With a futures or forward contract there is no payment of premiums to any one party or anything like that.

Let's take a look at the key factors that influence the price of futures and forwards to give us a better understanding into how they work. For a single stock future the underlying is the stock but for an equity index future the entire index is considered the underlying. Both work the same way but the key difference being the amount of stocks that influence the future, with a single stock future being influenced by just one single stock, and an equity index future being influenced by the aggregate price of the whole index.

Just as with any derivative, the price of the underlying stock or the index is the paramount concern in the pricing of futures. The current market price of the underlying along with dividends and interest rates are taken into consideration to determine the price of the futures contract. This simple formula can be used to give us an idea of how futures prices are determined:

Futures price = underlying stock (or index) price * (1+ the interest rate − dividends received)

The underlying stock or index price is always the start point and the price of the futures contract is based on that with adjustments for interest and dividends to ensure a "fair and reasonable" price between owning the futures contract and owning the underlying.

Dividends would be paid out on the underlying stock or the index between the time that the futures contract is bought and the time it matures. Someone holding the underlying index or single stock that the futures contract is derived from, gains the benefit of receiving dividends whereas futures contracts do not pay any dividends at all. Since dividends (representing earnings and are thus one of the most important influences on stock prices as we noted at the start) increase the stock price over time, a single stock (or index) that earns good dividends is desirable thus the price will tend to rise in the market. From the point of view of pricing a futures contract, it is not reasonable that the pricing of futures contracts include dividends to which futures contract holders are not entitled to receive. This is why dividends are subtracted as part of the pricing for futures contracts.

Now with dividends there is always a risk that they will not be paid before the futures contract matures. A company can simply cancel a dividend payment or reduce it and thus the holder of the underlying will miss out on that payment that was expected. Conversely, companies can increase the dividend payout and the futures contract holder would not have had that reflected in the price when he first bought the future. Changes in dividend payouts as the futures contract matures will cause the prices of the contracts to change. Thus, you can see how the dividends are reflected in the prices of futures.

Interest rates have a similar effect but these are added in to the price of the future. Futures are a leveraged product and you do not need to put up the full amount of capital to control a certain amount of shares. If someone were to buy the full stock index or the single stock which underlies the futures contract they would have to invest a large amount of capital to buy all the underlying shares for an equity index future or the single stock for a single stock future. This would require more capital than the futures holder needs and thus the futures holder is at an advantage. The futures holder is able to invest that excess capital that they did not use and earn a return on it, while at the same time holding the future on the index or the single stock. If you could earn interest plus have a position in a single stock or an equity index for the same amount of capital as it would take to buy the index or the single stock, then there is no point in buying the underlying shares in the first place as the future would always be a more efficient use of investing capital. Thus, for this reason, the interest rate is added to the cost of the futures contract to create more reasonable pricing compared to the underlying.

Just like with dividends, changes in interest rates will affect the price of the future. If the interest rate suddenly increased, the futures price will increase as the interest advantage for the futures holder is greater. Conversely, declining interest rates result in declining prices as there is less advantage for the futures holder. As both dividends and interest rates move, the price of the futures contract will move with them.

For a forward contract, interest rates and dividends will influence the price of the forward just as they would for a futures contract but it really depends on what the conditions and terms of the forward are. Since they are customized, there is a wide variety of forms that they can take and as such there are far more considerations for each counterparty. Outside of dividends and interest rates, one of the biggest concerns for any counterparty to a forward contract is the risk that the counterparty might not be able to uphold their end of the contract and either deliver the underlying or be able to pay for it when the contract matures. The pricing of forward contracts will reflect this; the more credit worthy a counterparty is perceived to be the better the pricing terms they may get in return.

So then let's take a look at how this all works at the broker dealer and how these are traded. A client has been reading some research reports and spoken to the research sales staff at the broker dealer over the last few days about ABC Inc. The client has become convinced that this stock is going to increase in price. They approach the broker dealer wanting to buy a futures contract for ABC Inc. The broker dealer will direct the client to the futures desk or the derivative desk that would handle exchange traded futures. The Delta One desk might also be a place where these are traded as we noted; it would depend on the structure of the broker dealer.

The client feels that the single stock ABC Inc. is going to go higher in the future so they buy a futures contract to get a price now as they expect it to be worth more in the future. There is a contact in the market for 100 shares of ABC Inc. at a price of $22.00 and it will mature in 3 months. This is just want the client needs so they buy 100 contracts (of 100 shares each) which total 10,000 shares.

This makes the total value of the contract $220,000 ($22.00 * 100 contracts * 100 shares each). However, as noted the client only needs to put up a small amount to cover this contract. The broker dealer offers this contract to the client with a margin requirement of 20%. This means that the client just needs to put up $44,000 to control a position of 10,000 shares worth $220,000. The client expects ABC Inc. to increase in price and they could have just bought the single stock, wait until it goes up and then sell it, but the buying the future is cheaper in terms of capital outlay. This concept of leverage is one of the key features of a futures contract. We saw this same thing with options which offer up leverage in a similar way.

The client buys these contracts and deposits the $44,000 with the broker dealer and pays the broker dealer commission for the futures purchase. For every futures contract bought, one is sold so somewhere in the market there is another 100 contracts sold by someone else who is the counter party. It is important to note that the number of counterparties can vary; perhaps there is just one counterparty with 100 contracts, or perhaps 5 counterparties with 20 contracts each. Just like with single stock cash equities, the number of counterparties and who they are does not matter and no one will ever know who the counterparties are. Regardless, for the purpose of this example, we will assume one counterparty with 100 contracts who has also deposited the margin amount of 20% with his broker dealer.

Each day the value of the futures contract to each party is calculated based on the price of ABC Inc. The day after the contract is bought the price of ABC Inc. declines to $21.00. This is now marked to market and the client's account total of $44,000 is debited $10,000 ($21.00-$22.00 = -$1.00 * 100 contracts * 100 shares) leaving $34,000 in the account. Likewise, the counterparty is credited with $10,000 ($22.00 – $21.00 = $1 * 100 contracts *100 shares). This flow of credits and debits on the margins put up by each counterparty will continue for as long as they hold the contracts. If the client was to have a few days of losses on the futures contract eventually the margin account will start to get depleted at which point the broker dealer will ask the client for more money to cover any more potential losses. Well luckily for the client, the price of ABC Inc. starts to rise and two weeks later the price hits $27.00 a share which means that the client's account would be credited with: $50,000 ($27.00-$22.00 = $5.00 * 100 contracts * 100 shares) and the total in the margin account is now $94,000. The client decides to get out of the position and take the profits now. In order to do so the client will need to offset their position. What this means is that they sell their futures contracts to another party in the market which they do and pay the broker dealer a commission for this trade.

So our client sells the position (since they were long to start with) and ends up with $94,000 in the account including the initial $44,000. This means that they made a profit of $50,000 with an investment of only $44,000. If the client had bought the 10,000 shares in the market at $22.00 at the start it would have cost them $220,000 and if they sold them at $27.00 a share they would have received: $270,000 which is also a $50,000 profit but it took a lot more capital to earn that profit. The use of the future offered them a lot of leverage to earn the same profit level with less capital used.

However, there is also a down side to using this leverage. The counterparty to the client would have lost $50,000 on this trade and they would end up owing money to their broker dealer. The initial deposit of $44,000 is not enough to cover the decline in value and the broker dealer would have asked them for more money to cover the trade as the value declined over time. At the end counterparty has lost their entire initial $44,000 and had to pay an additional $6,000 as well. It is important to remember that it is possible to lose more than you initially invested and actually owe more money in the end when trading futures.

The one final point to make is that in this example the price of the futures contract at the start was $22.00. The price of the underlying was never mentioned but in reality it would have differed from the price of the futures based on the impact of dividends and interest rates. The example compares the gains made on the futures trade to that of having bought the underlying shares. In reality the gains or losses between the two would not be exactly the same as the price of the underlying would be a little lower or higher than the price of the future but not substantially different so as to render the example invalid.

So having covered a futures trade let's take a look at a forward trade. A client contacts the broker dealer with a problem, they have a fund that they are closing down in 6 months and thus will need to liquidate the position across a number of different single stock shares. They are worried about future price declines on this portfolio so they want to secure a sale price now. After discussions with the transition management team, the client decides that they would like to enter into a forward contract with the broker dealer to help them secure a price for their portfolio now for delivery to the broker dealer in 6 months. The broker dealer considers entering into the forward contract with the client and from their side they begin to price the forward and determine what they can offer to the client. They look at this in consideration of their current inventory of shares that they have now and what will be coming in 6 months should they enter into this forward contract and agree to take delivery of them 6 months from now. They look at the prices now and look at the prices that they can expect in the future and how long they feel it will take to unload all these shares in the market with as little impact as possible. The broker dealer is mainly concerned with the price risk and market risk that might arise from taking delivery of the shares 6 months from now and will look for ways to hedge this risk with other products in the market perhaps using options or futures between now and the expected time of delivery.

The broker dealer comes back to the client with a price and terms and conditions. Both parties agree to the terms and they enter into the forward agreement. Unlike with a futures contract there are no deposits of money in the form of a margin as we saw with a futures contract. The forward contract is not marked to market everyday and no exchange of cash take place. In 6 months time the client will deliver the shares and the broker dealer will deliver the money as per the terms of the forward contract. Both parties will most likely hold the forward contract to maturity in 6 months time. The broker dealer does not charge any commission on this trade but instead will price in a "fee" into the price that they offer the client.

In reality the above example would probably be more complex than this but it does give you an idea of what would go on with a forward contract within the broker dealer and the general process each party would take.

• • •

17.2. Why do clients buy this product?

Hedging:

Futures and forward contracts offer clients ways to hedge existing positions or future positions in their investment portfolios. Entering into a contract allows one to fix the price now for a future that is uncertain. Thus the price risk can be removed or at least neutralized. This can also be used to protect profits as well as limit losses. When clients go short with a future they usually intend to sell a stock in the future and thus selling the future locks in the price and hedges against future price risk. Conversely, clients can use hedges to lock in a price of a stock that they want to buy in the future and one that is not yet part of their portfolio.

Hedging can also be used to keep a position in the market even if the portfolio manager does not have any position in the actual underlying shares or index. Given the leveraged nature of futures, the portfolio manager can create a sort of synthetic position by buying and or selling futures which is cheaper than actually investing the underlying stocks which would make up the portfolio normally. The leveraged nature of futures allows large value positions to be hedged with little use of capital.

Speculation:

Speculation is the other main reason clients use futures. The very risks that some clients seek to minimize can be exploited by another client seeking to speculate on the underlying stocks and equity indices. This all comes down to price speculations on the future price of a stock or an equity index. If a client feels that the price of a stock will rise in the future they will buy the contract now and as the contract matures and the price increases, the value of their position will increase. Conversely, for expected price declines they can sell the future now and see their position increase in value as time goes on and the stock price falls.

Futures can be really powerful if used correctly. It allows the clients to get higher returns compared to buying the underlying which would require a larger capital commitment. Price changes on futures contracts are magnified as a small change on the underlying translates into a larger change in the futures contract as it represents a greater number of shares. This means higher overall returns on the capital speculated with. Properly managed using the leverage contained, the futures contract offers the client ways to better use the investment capital they have at their disposal.

Eighteen

Equity Swaps

18.1. What are they?

An equity swap is an OTC derivative and as such falls into the execution portion of what a broker dealer offers to their clients. A swap is an exchange in which a set of future cash flows are periodically exchanged between two parties until some agreed on future date. The parties still hold their assets as these are not exchanged just the cash flows that the assets produce. These cash flows are known as "legs" and there is one for each party to the swap. One leg is pegged to the performance of a share of stock or the stock market index which functions as the underlying and the performance of that will determine the performance of that leg. The other leg is usually referenced against a floating interest rate, most commonly LIBOR and this is known as the floating leg of the swap. Let's take a look at what that is first as it plays a major role in understanding swaps.

LIBOR stands for the London Interbank Offered Rate which is an average of all the interest rates offered by banks to other banks. There are a set of member banks that provide an interest rate at which they are willing to lend and all these rates are averaged to come up with the LIBOR rate. These rates are calculated daily and cover various time periods from as short as an overnight rate to as long as a year. LIBOR acts as a reference rate for many fixed income products as well as its role in the equity swap as we will soon see.

So how does all this work then, what exactly are these swaps all about? Let's take a look at how this works at the broker dealer.

A hedge fund client contacts the broker dealer with interest in doing a swap. Just like any OTC derivative, there is always the risk that the counterparty might default or go bankrupt before the end of the swap and not be able to complete the transaction. Likewise, the broker dealer faces the same risk with the client. However, the client has faith in the broker dealer based on its credit rating and the broker dealer has been a trusted partner in the past and a large player in the market so the client is comfortable dealing with them.

The client will most likely be directed to the Delta One desk where most broker dealers situate trading in swaps. The client explains that they would like to find a way to gain some exposure to an underlying equity index and inquire about what swaps the broker dealer might be able to engage in as counterparty. They have $10 million in cash to commit to this. Each swap agreement is governed by standardized documentation setup by the International Swap and Derivatives Association (ISDA). These agreements provide the standard clauses and conditions and the participants to a swap will fill in the agreement with their terms and conditions such as the amounts and time period.

The client and the broker dealer discuss the terms and the broker dealer comes back with an offer. The client is agreeable and the standardized ISDA agreement is signed. The terms they agree to are; that they will enter into a swap for a notional principal amount of $10 million for a period of 2 years and the exchange of payments will be made every 6 months. The rate they agree to is LIBOR +1%. The 6 month LIBOR rate is currently 4% so this makes the total rate 5% for the floating leg that the client will take responsibility for. The index that the broker dealer is responsible for is currently at 2,000. The swap is agreed to, the contracts signed and the first payment is

6 months out. In 6 months time the index is at 2100. This would be the payment scenario for each party:

The broker dealer would need to pay to the client: 2,100 (the index level now) / 2,000 the index level at the start * $10,000,000. This totals: $500,000

The client would need to pay to the broker dealer: 10,000,000 * 182 days (which is considered the first 6 months) / 356 days * 5%. This totals: $249,315.

In this payment swap the broker dealer loses out as the index has increased in price and thus the payment to the client was larger than that the client paid to the broker dealer.

Six months later the next payment is due and the index has declined to 1,950. This would be the payment scenario for each party:

From the broker dealer's point of view the index has declined: 1,950/2100 (notice how the index rate used is that at the time of the payment 6 months ago). This indicates a decline of: 7.14%. The broker dealer does not have to pay anything since the "cash flow" is negative and there is no return.

The client would need to pay to the broker dealer two things in this case since the index has declined. First there is the fixed payment determined by the interest rate: $10,000,000 * 183 days (which is considered the last 6 months) / 356 days x 5%. This totals: $250,684.

In addition, the client will have to pay to make up for the decline in the index which had a negative return. This is the main risk the client took on when they entered the swap. They are exchanging a set of fixed payment amounts for the opportunity to participate in the index. This creates a synthetic position in that the client does not actually own the index in the form of an ETF or a group of stocks that would provide the same returns but they get to participate as if they owned the index earning both positive and possibly negative returns. The client had expected that the index would increase over the life of the swap and increase by more than they had to pay in fixed payments. In this case it did not so they have to pay the difference: $10,000,000 * the percentage decline in the index of 7.14% = $714,000. Thus the total payment to the broker dealer is the regular fixed amount of: $250,684 and the payment based on the decline in the value of the index of: $714,000 for a total of: $964,684.

So far for the year the exchange of payments for the broker dealer is $500,000 and $1,213,999 for the client. The client is now hoping that the index will increase in the second year of the swap so that they can hopefully make back the money that they lost. Perhaps the client might not want to face that risk over the next year and terminate the contract. Fortunately there are ways that this can be done.

Depending on the terms of the swap contract, both parties might be able to terminate the contract as long as the other agrees. This termination clause would have discussed when the contract was first negotiated. Should that clause be in the contract, the client would be able to terminate the contract settling the payments owed and accepting the loss.

Alternatively, the client can enter into another swap agreement that offsets the first with the client receiving the fixed payments and having to pay out based on the return of the index. This could be negotiated with another broker dealer or perhaps even with the same broker dealer the client did the original swap with if that broker dealer is agreeable to it of course.

The client could also sell the swap to another counterparty. The new counterparty would replace the client in the agreement. This would of course have to be allowable in the swap contract at the start. However, in this case it might be hard for the client to find another counterparty given that the swap is at a loss right now. The broker dealer would be in a better position than the client is to exit the swap contract in this manner.

In addition to the sample swap above, there are plenty of other swaps available between different assets. They can be customized to meet client requirements as needed and as long as there is a willing and acceptable counterparty available there is almost no limit to the combinations available.

• • •

18.2. Why do clients buy this product?

Cost:

Owning shares comes with costs even if they are not being traded. Shares that are held by clients have to be held with a custodian and this means paying fees to that custodian to take care of the holdings. Corporate actions on stocks occur from time to time and these need to be attended to and records maintained. All this requires back office staff to provide these support services for these holdings. Equity swaps provide the benefit in that a client can gain exposure to equities as part of the swap without having to actually hold any equities. They can simply pay a fixed percentage and receive payments influenced by the performance of equities.

Synthetic Positions:

As we saw with the example above, a swap creates an artificial or synthetic position. This can be beneficial as it can allow investors access to markets that they would not otherwise have access to. For example, there are some emerging markets that clients want access to but these markets have capital controls in place that limit investment or control it. A swap could be a way for the client to gain exposure to that market without having to actually hold stocks in that market.

Voting Rights and Ownership:

Swaps can be used to hedge a position in a stock without losing the voting rights. Since the actual assets are not exchanged the owner still holds the equities and owns the voting rights. A client could enter into a swap agreement for a set of securities that they believe are going to decline in value exchanging the return on those securities for a fixed payment. The client does not want to sell these stocks even though they expect them to decline in value in the near time because they wish to maintain the voting rights. Should the securities decline in value during the life of the swap, the client has successfully hedged the decline and at the same time retained the voting rights in the securities.

Ninteen

Warrants

19.1. What are they?

A warrant is a derivative security that entitles the holder to buy or sell the underlying common stock of the issuing company at a certain predetermined price for a certain set period of time. On the surface this sounds like a call option and indeed warrants have a lot in common with options as we will soon see. Warrants are issued by corporations usually when a company either issues debt or equity, such as when the company issues preferred shares.

As we know, preferred shares have a first call on the dividends of the company and some preferred shares actually come with specific dividend payouts. Warrants are issued alongside the preferred shares to make the issue more attractive in what is known as a "sweetener". Companies hope that they can issue the preferred shares with a lower dividend payout as the warrant will make the issue more attractive to investors compared to preferred shares from other companies that might have higher dividend payouts. The use of a warrant can also encourage investors to take advantage and buy the shares should the price be favourable and increase their investment in the firm. From the company's point of view this is a win win situation for them, they are able to issue lower dividend paying preferred shares and encourage more investment in their firm via the warrant.

Companies will also sometimes issue warrants as part of a debt issue. When debt is issued and sold to investors, warrants are sometimes issued along with the debt for the same reason as with preferred shares. The addition of a warrant allows the firm to offer up a lower interest rate to the investors than other possible competing bond issues. Interest payments on debt and dividend payments on preferred shares are fixed costs that the company must pay out and the lower these are the better it is for the firm and thus the warrant helps companies achieve that. Once the warrant is issued as part of a preferred share or debt issuance they are able to be separated out and sold and traded separately. The holder of the warrant who received it initially as part of the debt or equity issuance is able to sell these on the market to others. For those purchasing warrants it is important to note that they do not own the underlying stock and are not entitled to dividends on the stock.

So then how do these warrants work? To start with, there are two types of warrants; a call warrant and a put warrant. A call warrant allows the holder the right to buy a certain amount of the underlying shares at a specific price known as the strike price from the issuer at time prior to expiry. In this sense they are exactly the same as a call option. A put warrant gives the holder an option to sell a certain amount of the underlying at a specific price back to the issuer at a time prior to expiry. Both put and call warrants have European and American "styles" to them in that European warrants can only be used at expiry and American warrants can but used at any time prior to expiry.

The prices of warrants traded in the secondary market after they have been issued are influenced by the same factors as options; price of the underlying, price volatility of the underlying, dividends, the risk free interest rate and of course the concepts of intrinsic value and time value. Again warrants look exactly the same as call and put options right down to what influences their prices however, there are a few key differences to consider.

The biggest difference is that the warrants are created by the issuing company whereas options are products created by the exchanges on which they trade and the company that issued the underlying is not involved with their creation. With options both parties (the buyers and sellers) are market participants but with a warrant the issuing company is always a party to the agreement. If you hold a call warrant and exercise it the issuing company delivers the shares to you. If you hold a put warrant and exercise it the issuing company buys the shares from you. The issuing company is always counterparty to the warrant holder. Any shares that end up getting delivered from the exercise of a call warrant are newly created shares that are created by the issuing company. With a put warrant the shares are returned to the issuing company. The exercise of warrants changes the number of outstanding shares in the market for that particular stock. When an option is exercised the movement of shares occurs between two parties and does not affect the total number of outstanding shares available in the market which remains unchanged, only the owners change.

Options are traded on exchanges and as such they are standardized products. They have set expiry dates and cycles such as the third Saturday of the month as we saw with US exchange listed options. Options usually have expiry periods that last up to 8 months, even the longest option contract available, known as LEAPs (Long-term Equity Anticipation Securities), only have expiries up to 3 years from their initial issuance.

Warrants, on the other hand, can have expiry dates stretching on for years, up until 15 years in some cases. Since warrants are usually issued as part of a debt or equity issue there are no standardized expiry dates or cycles. Warrants are by their nature customized products and are generally traded as OTC products although some warrants are registered by the issuing company and will trade on exchanges.

Let's now take a look at an example of how a warrant works.

The stock ABC Incorporated is currently trading at $20.50 a share. Analysts at the broker dealer feel it is going to go much higher in the next 1 to 2 years, probably as high as $35-$40 a share. One of the research sales staff reads this research because he knows that one of his big clients is interested in taking a position in ABC Incorporated. He comes up with a trading idea involving the use of warrants on ABC Inc.'s stock however these are only traded over the counter and not on an exchange. Working with derivatives traders, he finds warrants costing $1.00 a warrant and the issuing company will sell the shares to the warrant holders at strike price of $34.00. The warrants have been trading in the secondary market for a few years and they have 3 years left on them before they expire. He calls his client and pitches the trading idea to buy the warrants and use them to hopefully make a profit.

This warrant is currently out of the money and has no intrinsic value but the client trusts the analyst to be correct as he has in the past and agrees to buy warrants for 100 shares on ABC Incorporated (the underlying) paying $100 ($1.00 a warrant on 100 shares) to the current holder of the warrants.

The research salesperson and the client who bought the warrants watch the stock price of ABC over the next few months. Six months after the client bought the warrants the share price on ABC Incorporated declines to $15.00 and the warrants are now even more "out of the money" as the price of the underlying is below the strike price.

A year has passed since the warrants were first bought and now the share price is $34.00 which makes it "at the money" as the strike price equals the underlying price and now the client could exercise the warrants to buy the shares from the issuer and the issuer will have to issue those shares and give them to the client. However, the client can buy the shares in the open market for the same price instead of having to use the warrant so the warrant still has no intrinsic value (warrants have the same concept of intrinsic value that we saw with options) as follows underlying price ($34.00) − the strike price ($34.00) = intrinsic value ($0.00). The client holds on to the warrant as it still has two years left and that is a lot of time for the price of the underlying to move.

Another six months pass and the price is now $35.00 a share. The warrant is still "in the money" as the strike price was $34.00. The strike price is less than the underlying now and we have intrinsic value of $1.00 a share as follows: the underlying price ($35.00) − the strike price ($34.00) = intrinsic value ($1.00) meaning that the warrant has real value now. However the client is still not going to make any money as he had to pay $1.00 a share for the warrants so the client is only just going to break even so they hold off exercising it. Of course the goal is to make a profit and with 1.5 years left on the warrant the client is going to wait. It is important to note that the premium for these warrants would have increased in the market as it is now in the money and anyone buying these same warrants now that the client bought at the start would pay a higher premium.

Six months later the price suddenly starts to go up just as the analyst was predicting. The price hits $40.00 a share. The client chooses to exercise the warrant for the 100 shares and pays the issuer the strike price of $34.00 a share for 100 shares for a total of $3,400 making their total cost $3,500 considering the $100 cost for the warrants already paid. The client takes possession of the shares from the issuer and then instructs the broker dealer to sell the 100 shares at $40.00 a share for a total of $4,000 making a profit of $500. The client could have potentially waited another year as the warrant still had one year to go until expiry and see if the price of the underlying increased further but instead of taking the risk that the price could drop they exercised the warrants and took their profits. Instead of exercising the warrants the client could have simply sold them to another buyer in the market.

From the broker dealer's point of view, they would have made a commission on the sale of the warrants to the client. With warrants there is no way for the broker dealer to enter into a trade as counterparty. With an option the broker dealer could setup a customized option with client and act as counterparty to that trade and thus price in their "fee" into the trade. Warrants only ever have the issuer as counterparty to whoever holds the warrant. Broker dealers can act as market maker for warrants and create a secondary market for the trading of warrants and thus make money off the bid ask spread and of course any trading commissions on the purchase and sale of them.

• • •

19.2. Why do clients buy this product?

Hedging:

Much like with options, warrants can be used to hedge positions in the same ways as with options. The only thing to consider when doing this is that options are usually more liquid and easier to trade compared to a warrant but aside from that the same basic hedging concepts covered in the section on options apply here as well.

Leverage:

Much the same as with options, warrants give the buyer leverage to control the same number of shares but with less capital cost or to control a much larger number of shares for the same capital cost. As with the leverage concepts covered in the section on options, the same apply here.

Twenty

Convertible Bonds

20.1. What are they?

A convertible bond straddles both the equity and fixed income worlds in that it is a bond that can be converted to stock in the company. Much like with an option or a warrant, there is a "strike price" known as the "conversion price" that dictates when the bond holder can convert the bond into shares, a process we will look at a little later. The convertible nature of the bond allows the holder to receive interest income like they would with a bond and at the same time have the option to participate in any increases in the price of the underlying equity by converting it to equity and then selling those shares in the market once the conversion is favorable. However, convertible bonds usually have a feature that allows the issuing company to force the conversion of the bond to equity shares in the issuing company at a certain price. This limits the upside in price that a convertible bond holder can possibly gain.

Before we take a look in detail at the product, we need to first take a look at some of the basic bond concepts. Bonds are as we noted in the start of the book, are the second way that companies raise funds along with equity. With a bond you are simply loaning money to a corporation and the corporation will pay you interest on the bond over time and once the bond matures you will receive the amount that you loaned them returned to you. Here is a brief example of this concept; ABC Inc. issues a bond with a maturity of 10 years with a coupon (rate of interest on the bond) of 5% with a face value of $100. Face value is also known as "par value" and is used to calculate the interest payments and the amount that will be returned at maturity. So with this bond we can expect $5 a year in interest ($5 for each $100 as $100 * 0.05 = $5) and at maturity the $100 we lent will be repaid. It is important to note that par value and the market price of a bond will differ and they are not the same. When the bond is first issued the "price" at that time is the face value, investors hand over $100 for each bond and will expect $100 in return once the bond matures (if they still own it then) and the interest payments as well. However, just like with stocks, bonds can be sold and bought to and from others and the market price of the bond will change in comparison to the par value. Just like with stocks, there are several factors that influence the price of a bond but the most important is the interest rate. In our example above the bond is paying 5% but if the interest rates in the market fall and other bonds are now only paying 4% then the bond we have will increase in price because it pays a higher rate of interest than others thus making it more desirable. We might see the price increase to $101 or $102 for par value of $100 which would mean that our bond is trading at a premium in comparison to the par value. Conversely, if interest rates increase over time, the price of the bond we have will fall to perhaps $99 or $98 and our bond will be trading at a discount to the par value. The exact price relationship between interest rates and the price of bonds is complex and not the main topic of this book but it is important to understand this concept when looking at convertible bonds. In the end, regardless of how much someone paid for a bond the par value is the value that they will get once the bonds matures. So in the case of the ABC Inc. bond the value returned at maturity is $100.

Par value also comes into play with the conversion of the convertible bond into shares in the company. The conversion price and the par value are used to calculate the conversion ratio. Let's take a look at that same bond from ABC Inc. but this time it is a convertible bond with a 10 year maturity, a coupon of 5%, a face or par value of $100, a conversion price of $25.00 and the current stock price is $19.95. The conversion of the bond to equity cannot happen until the stock price reaches $25.00. This means that once the price of the underlying stock reaches $25.00 the holder of the bond can convert it into shares. The conversion of the bond into shares is determined by the ratio between the par value and the conversion price. Divide the par value of the bond with the conversion price and you get the conversion ratio which in this case is $100 divided by $25.00, which means that for each $100 of the bond we will get 4 equity shares. It is important to note that the conversion price can change depending on certain conditions like a corporate change of control event but so this example let's keep it simple.

Now that we have an idea of how they work, let's take a look at what influences their prices. The valuation of convertible bonds in the market is complex because as a hybrid product the markets need to consider both the bond and the equity aspect of these products. For the bond component, as we noted, interest rates have a large impact on the price of bonds. However, in addition to this there are other factors that influence the price of the bond that we will just cover briefly here. The credit rating of the firm influences the price of bonds. Generally, the higher the credit rating of the firm the better the chance that it will be able to pay its obligations thus, as a firm's credit rating increases, the price of its bonds will increase as they are more desirable compared to those of companies with lower credit ratings. Conversely, lowered credit ratings reduce bond prices. Finally, the concept of duration of the bond until maturity needs to be looked at as it is important in the valuations for bond prices. The longer the maturity of the bond, the longer the investor's need to wait until the principal is repaid. Duration is linked to interest rates and thus as interest rates go up, the price of bonds with longer durations will fall faster than those with shorter durations and vice versa. The concept of duration is a lot more complex then this but for the purposes we are trying to cover this should be sufficient.

For the equity portion, the valuation is treated the same as that for a warrant; the price of the underlying, the volatility of the price, the dividends paid on the common stock and interest rates. These same factors work the same way with warrants as they do with the equity portion of a convertible bond. Just as we saw with options and warrants; the terminology of "in, at and out of the money" apply to the convertible bond. A convertible bond is:

In the money: when the conversion price is less than the price of the underlying equity.
At the money: when the conversion price is equal to the price of the underlying equity.
Out of the money: when the conversion price is greater than the price of the underlying equity.

As the price of the underlying stock approaches the conversion price, the price of the convertible bond traded in the market will increase as well. The valuation of the equity portion will become increasingly important as this happens. Conversely, if the price of the underlying is trading far below the conversion price, then the value of the equity portion will be near zero as it has no value and the convertible bond will be valued just like other bonds are without much consideration to the equity portion.

Now that we have covered what convertible bonds are and how they are valued, let's look at why companies issue them. The biggest reason for issuing a convertible bond much like with a warrant, is that the convertible aspect of the bond could be considered a sweetener as it allows the buyer of the bond the option to convert the bond to shares in the company and participate in any stock price increases that they would not otherwise have access to as a bond owner. This means that the issuing company can issue a convertible bond for a lower rate of interest than a normal bond. For a company this can mean a lot of savings in interest payments over the life of the bond. However, it is important to note that while convertible bonds are generally considered less secure compared to other bonds they rank ahead preferred shares and common shares if a company goes bankrupt.

Another reason for a company to issue convertible bonds is because convertible bonds allow the company to delay share dilution. Dilution is when a company issues new shares on top of the existing ones in the market. This means that the total volume of shares increases and an existing shareholder's portion is reduced. Let's say that a company has 10,000 shares and you own 5,000 of them. Well in effect you own half of the company. The company has total earnings of $10,000 which it distributes to each shareholder at $1 per share. You would be entitled to $5,000 in dividend income. If the company then issues a further 5,000 shares the total would be 15,000 shares outstanding. Your percentage of ownership is "diluted" to 33% as you only own 5,000 of the total outstanding 15,000 shares. The company's earnings are still $10,000 but now they are spread across 15,000 shares which means that each share only earns $0.66 per share now so your total dividends are "diluted" to $3,333 instead of the $5,000 you received before the issuance of more shares.

Since the company has issued a convertible bond instead of shares the dilution of the share ownership and the earnings per share can be "postponed" until the company's earnings have increased enough to "support" the dilution of shares. As we noted at the start of this book, a company's stock price will increase as its earnings increase thus the price of the stock will naturally increase possibly triggering the conversion of bond into shares at a level when the company can pay out the same level of earnings. The company could also arrange for a force conversion to equity at a time that is convenient for them using the convertible bond, of course this condition would have to be included in the bond when it was first issued.

• • •

20.2. Why do clients buy this product?

Flexibility:

From a client's point of view, the main reason to buy them is that they offer the safe income of a bond but the chance to participate in the upside of the underlying equity. There are of course limits to this, the bond's interest rate as noted is generally lower than non convertible bonds and the equity participation will be capped as there will be a maximum price that the stock can rise to before the conversion is forced but these are small prices to pay for the flexibility that this hybrid product provides. In addition, the convertible bond is a bond and thus it ranks higher in terms of repayment in the event of a bankruptcy then preferred or common shares giving the investor exposure to the equity with the safety of the fixed income investment in the event of a bankruptcy.

Arbitrage:

Convertible bonds also attract the attention of clients of the broker dealer especially hedge funds who like to engage in what is known as convertible arbitrage. This strategy seeks to make profit on any mispricing between the price of the convertible bond and price of the underlying common stock. If the bond appears to be undervalued compared to the stock, the bond will be bought and the stock will be sold short. The idea is that the market will soon "correct" this mis-valuation and the price of the bond will rise and the price of the stock will fall all things being equal. This allows a client taking this position to make a profit on the increasing bond price and at the same time make a profit on the falling stock price. Such arbitrage can be very complex because you are dealing with a lot of factors that influence the prices of both the equity and bond parts of the product.

Twenty One

Proprietary Trading

21.1. What is it?

Well here we are at the last section of the book and the last "product" of the broker dealer. However, this is where things become a little different and why we left this to last because generally there is no client involved. Proprietary Trading is what is known as a "principal" business in that the broker dealer is dealing strictly with their own capital. This is not a business with the broker dealer acting as an agent for the client so for the most part the term "broker" need not apply. The proprietary trading area of the broker dealer is usually called "the prop desk" which engages in "prop trading".

The desk is an area within the broker dealer that sits on the trading floor but is usually kept away from the agency sales traders. They are usually segregated off from the agency traders by what are known as "Chinese Walls". This same concept is used to keep the investment banking division away from the broker dealer division so that information about clients' capital raising activities are not divulged to sales traders who could in turn advise clients on upcoming activity in a certain stock that would allow them to make a profit. The prop desk is isolated from both the investment banking division and the rest of the broker dealer division for reasons of conflicts of interest between the clients when the broker dealer acts as a broker and agent and when the broker dealer acts as a dealer using its own capital. If the prop traders know what the clients are interested in then they can trade based on the information. For example, if a prop trader knows that a client is interested in buying a large amount of a certain stock then the prop trader can buy that stock ahead of time in anticipation of the rise in price caused by the client's order. Likewise, with a sell order that will depress the price, the prop trader could short sell the stock. This is known as front running and is illegal as a practice.

The prop trader's day is much like that of a sales trader, they start the morning early and have a morning meeting on the developments in the market the previous day and activities in other markets overnight. They also review the positions on their books and prepare for the day's trading. Each prop trader will have a "book" or an account with a certain amount of capital provided by the firm that they are allowed to use in trading. As they buy and sell stocks, they will first create and then later exit positions and this is reflected in their trading book. The book will contain the most important statistic of all; known as "P&L" which means "profit and loss". Unlike with agency traders, there are no sales commissions and the profits the prop desk makes are solely from the increasing values in the positions that they hold. These values are in real time and are constantly changing throughout the day. In the early morning before the markets open, the prop trader will review the P&L and see where each positions sits and the overall value of the book. They will plan out their trades and get some idea of what they want to trade during the day either getting out of positions by selling them or taking on new positions.

The prop trader functions as an execution trader as well. A lot of them can do their own executions especially for trades that they feel are important. Likewise, just like with agency sales and execution traders, they can access the algorithm system and put trades into that system to be traded. The broker dealer will have developed customized algorithms for use in their prop trading activities that may differ from the ones offered to their agency clients.

Prop traders will trade on positions for the short term usually anything from a few seconds to a couple of days. Also, they will look at longer term trends and try to play them out as well. There is no one set way to try to make a profit in the markets. In addition to buying and selling stocks, prop traders are free to use all the other instruments like options, futures and other derivatives that we have covered in this book. With no clients to dictate the trades, prop traders have freedom to engage in a lot of different trades. However, since they are playing with the broker dealer's money, there is a lot more responsibility involved as positions can quickly turn into losses if not managed properly. Thus, they will try to hedge a lot of their positions to protect profits already earned or to limit potential losses.

Risk management is a big part of the role that they do, after all no one wants to be remembered as the person who brought down the bank due to bad trades. To mitigate this, the team of prop traders usually work and trade together with a shared risk amount. This encourages communication between the traders and helps to eliminate the possibility that one trader trading in isolation has gotten into a bad position. Risk is measured is what is known as; VAR or "value at risk". This measure is composed of three components; the potential amounts that could be lost, the probability of that loss occurring and the time frame that this probability might take place in. This is calculated on the total value of the portfolio and is usually expressed as a percentage chance of a loss, such as a 5% chance per day that a portfolio will fall by $5,000,000. This means that the model assumes that this will eventually happen. In fact a 5% chance means this will happen once in every 20 days or about once a month.

So that about covers what proprietary trading is all about but there is one other aspect that we want to cover and return to; recall how we discussed market making and facilitation? Well this is where the line between broker and dealer can become a little blurry. Depending on the firm and the structure of the firm, the prop desk could be involved in market making and facilitation activities for clients. Since facilitation involves the broker dealer taking a position as counterparty for the client, the prop desk is sometimes tasked with this since they are the ones dealing with the broker dealer's own capital. This can make it hard to determine where pure prop trading and market making are divided and how any conflicts of interest can be resolved. This was another issue that was raised during the Volcker rule discussions.

Twenty Two

Conclusion

I hope that you have learned something from this book. There has been a lot to cover and a lot of it is interrelated as nothing exists in isolation. I have tried to convey the most important concepts and how they are applied within the broker dealer industry. However, it is impossible to capture every little detail and every possible product within this complex world. Indeed, I do not know them all myself but I hope that by sharing my knowledge I have given you an insight to the world of equities. Thank you for purchasing this book and taking the time to read it.

www.ingramcontent.com/pod-product-compliance
Lightning Source LLC
Chambersburg PA
CBHW051526170526
45165CB00002B/621